Bowhunting Pressured Whitetails

John Eberhart and Chris Eberhart

STACKPOLE BOOKS

Published by
STACKPOLE BOOKS
5067 Ritter Road
Mechanicsburg, PA 17055
www.stackpolebooks.com

Printed in U.S.A.

10 9 8 7 6 5 4 3 2

First edition

Cover design by Wendy Reynolds
Cover photograph by Len Rue, Jr.

Library of Congress Cataloging-in-Publication Data

Eberhart, John.
  Bowhunting pressured whitetails / John Eberhart and Chris Eberhart.—1st ed.
    p. cm.
  ISBN 0-8117-2819-6 (pbk.)
  1. White-tailed deer hunting. 2. Bowhunting. I. Eberhart, Chris. II. Title.
  SK301.E33 2003

799.2'7652—dc21
2002156073

Contents

Acknowledgments

Without the help of many fine people, this book never would have been written. We thank our entire family for their support and patience. Gayleen, thank you for your patience and help with writing. Susi, thank you for your patience and for allowing time and a place to write. Jon, you are truly a brilliant hunter, and without your suggestions and long hours together with us in the woods, this book never would have taken its current form. We learn much from you. To our grandsons and nephews, we look forward to the day when we will hunt together.

Many friends have helped us with this project. It is impossible to list every person who had some part in our learning to hunt, but those people, whether they know it or not, were integral to the creation of this book. To all of those hunters out there who have shared bits of knowledge with us through the years, we say thank you. Thanks to Chad Stearns, Ed Simpson, Randy Williams, Tom Whitfield, and Terry Kemp for proofreading and critiquing our manuscript. You are all excellent hunters, and all of your suggestions were carefully considered. We thank Chris Dilley for sharing his insight, listening to our story, and setting an example. Thanks also to Jack Van Ripper for allowing us to use some of your live deer photographs.

Introduction

Hunting means many things to many people. For some, it is a form of relaxation; for others, it is a means of obtaining food; and for still others, it is a vital component of the fabric of existence. For my father, John Eberhart, and me, hunting is an almost necessary part of living. There have been seasons when I was not able to hunt, but in those years I was unbearable, as my friends and family will attest. Likewise for my father, for whom it would be difficult, at best, to live in a world without hunting. It was he who taught me how to hunt. He taught me as he was learning and is still learning. There were never any absolutes in his hunting method, which sometimes made learning difficult. In the early years, I just tagged along, watching and trying to pick up on some of the clues that made my father such a successful hunter. I watched, learned, and made slow progress in developing both skill and success.

In the early years, I was a child just struggling to see and shoot deer. Later, after a few successes, I was a more effective hunter, but I still did not have a clue about what I was doing. As a few more years passed, I started to understand what bowhunting was about, and success has come more easily, though it is still an amazingly difficult challenge. I know my father's hunting methods intimately and watched many of them develop throughout the years. Learning to hunt is a progression that never stops. When you think you know everything, learning stops and stagnation sets in. This happens to most hunters at some point; however, it has yet to happen to my father, who tries to learn something new on every hunt. The methods presented here are the result of his forty-plus years of intense hunting and learning. Though I know his methods well and hunt in the same manner, he deserves all the credit. Without him, I would surely hunt differently, perhaps not at all.

Writing is another story. This book is a project that began several years ago. Through general dissatisfaction with the information appearing in hunting magazines, my father started writing articles for small regional magazines in the late eighties. This, however, he did at a leisurely pace and purely out of interest in hunting. Though he had talked about writing a book for years, it would have taken him decades to write an entire book at his normal pace, which is slowed by a full and hectic work schedule and numerous other commitments. Knowing the unique quality of his hunting style, and the benefit it would bring other hunters in areas where competition is fierce, I decided to take the project in hand.

I first took all existing material and organized it in logical order, then filled in the gaps with new chapters. In these chapters, I used my father's voice and his hunting stories as he told them to me. I also revised all the existing material, making everything fit together in a more coherent fashion. After a draft was created, my father and I spent unbelievable amounts of time refining the elements of each chapter several times, until we could agree on both content and style. Sometimes this process was painful for both of us. Some sentences just did not want to fit, and some detail was nearly impossible to relay without writing another book entirely. We were forced to articulate aspects of hunting that we had taken for granted, and we had to work together very closely, which is something that is not always so easy for our very independent souls.

This book is the result of these joint efforts. We hope you will gain as much from reading it as we did from writing it. It is designed for people who have hunting circumstances similar to ours and are faced with a great deal of hunting pressure. It is for hunters in average situations who want to become better bowhunters and enjoy consistent success on mature bucks—or any buck, for that matter—in pressured areas. Of course, any hunting tactic that works well on pressured deer will work even better in areas with little hunting pressure. With some hard work, discipline, and a lot of patience, you can become a successful bowhunter of mature bucks no matter where you hunt.

C. E.

CHAPTER 1

Pressured Bucks

A whitetail buck is a whitetail buck, right? Wrong. Deer, like people, are born into different sets of circumstances. Some deer happen to be born in areas that see tremendous hunting pressure; others are born in areas with little or no hunting pressure. This naturally has an effect on their behavior. It is similar to the differences in behavior between humans born and raised in an inner-city setting and those born and raised in a rural area. Though people are people no matter where they live, their reactions to certain stimuli are largely influenced by their environment. The same thing occurs with deer.

The majority of deer in many states, such as Michigan, Pennsylvania, New York, West Virginia, Kentucky, and Mississippi, to name just a few, experience hunting pressure probably as heavy as it gets. Although basic deer behavior remains the same, bucks that grow to maturity in areas where hunter numbers per square mile are high could almost be considered a different breed of animal. They have had contact with hunters trying to kill them their entire lives, beginning while barely out of their spots. The bucks that reach maturity in these and many other hard-hunted areas around the country have been conditioned to hunters. The mature bucks pay close attention to their surroundings, and when there is any hint of human presence, they seem to just disappear. In many areas of heavy hunting, the mature buck is almost an enigma.

States with extreme hunting pressure also have a relatively high human population. Here the average size of private-property parcels is relatively small compared with that in less heavily hunted states. The reason for this is simple: With more people, there is more competition for land, thus leading to greater property fragmentation and higher prices. It is not uncommon in my home state of Michigan to hunt on parcels of five to twenty acres. In less populated big-buck states, most parcels I have received permission to hunt on were at least a hundred acres, and some were more than a thousand acres. The difference in property fragmentation creates two distinct situations.

In highly populated states, it is common to have twenty or more property owners in each section (one square mile, or 640 acres), and up to thirty different landowners in a section is not unusual even in rural areas. If every one of the twenty or thirty landowners allows two or three people to hunt on his or her property, this means most sections will have an absolute minimum of forty hunters, and sometimes fifty or more. More than likely about half of them will bowhunt, but they'll all be out there on opening day of gun season.

Opening morning of the 1978 Michigan gun season was a day I will always remember. After the crack of daylight, I was hearing so many shots that I decided to count seconds between them. I would start counting after a shot and count until the next shot was fired. Between 7:30 and 9:30 A.M., I never counted more than thirteen seconds between them. That much gun-hunting pressure conditions deer for the rest of their lives, if they survive past that day. Sometimes it seems as if there are more deer hunters per square mile than deer. It is no wonder that with so many hunters, few bucks make it to maturity in these highly pressured areas. And this is not an uncommon situation.

Every once in a while in these hard-hunted areas, someone kills a magnificent buck. The locals, who are convinced a deer of such caliber could not possibly live in their neighborhood, are generally quite surprised and assume the buck must have wandered in from another area during the rut. This occasional big buck is proof that mature bucks are out there. It is also proof that they have been so well conditioned to hunters and hunters' methods that it is almost impossible to kill them using ordinary hunting techniques.

On the other hand, there are many areas with fewer hunters and less fragmented land, where deer encounter little or no hunting pressure. In these areas, bucks have a chance to live to maturity with little disturbance. And if they are hunted, there is already a balanced age structure in the herd that makes yearling bucks, and quite often two-and-a-half-year-old bucks, not very interesting to local or visiting hunters, thus allowing them to live. These bucks still associate hunters with danger, but because of the scarcity of hunters pursuing them, they move much more regularly during daylight hours than those in heavily hunted areas. Areas like these are vast in some states, among them Iowa (where I have hunted four times), Kansas, Nebraska, Illinois, the Dakotas, and Montana, as well as all of the Canadian provinces.

I am speaking generally here, and there are exceptions to all of this. There are small pockets with heavy hunting pressure even in the most lightly hunted regions with overall low hunter numbers. And in the most heavily hunted states, there are large tracts of land, such as hunt clubs or properties bordering no-hunting zones, that have very little or severely regulated hunting pressure.

Look in any hunting magazine, and you'll see that most writers and the vast majority of articles about big-buck kills come from areas with a lack of hunting pressure, where there is a much higher mature buck-to-doe ratio. Mature bucks in these regions are simply much easier to get close to and kill. Have you ever wondered why there are so few big names in modern whitetail bowhunting who trophy-hunt in heavily hunted states like Pennsylvania, New York, Michigan, Kentucky, and Mississippi? It's not that the hunters in Iowa, Illinois, Nebraska, or Kansas are better, but that it is simply easier to kill big bucks in some areas than it is in others.

The table below lists the number of deer bowhunting licenses sold in selected states and provinces in 1998, the number of whitetail bucks from each state entered into the Pope and Young (P & Y) record book that year, and the ratio of these record bucks to hunters. A handful of states have much lower hunter-to-record-buck ratios. Assuming the rate of entry into the record books is the same in all the listed states, it should be obvious that killing mature bucks in those states is much easier than in other states farther down the list. In fact, your odds of bagging a P & Y buck in one of the top four states is ten to twenty times greater than in some of the hard-hunted states. This is a pretty good guide if you are considering hunting outside of your home state. Wisconsin is an interesting exception. This state has considerable hunting pressure yet maintains an outstanding hunter-to-record-buck ratio. I believe this can be attributed to several different unique circumstances, including intense agriculture, special terrain features along the Mississippi River, and the practice of quality deer management for many years. Wisconsin consistently places about twice as many P & Y bucks in the book each year as the next closest state.

State or Province	Bowhunting Licenses Sold[†]	P & Y Bucks Entered[†]	Ratio	
Iowa	36,800	145	1 :	253
Kansas	17,800	69	1 :	257
Illinois	86,769	236	1 :	367
Nebraska[*]	18,235	49	1 :	372

State or Province	Bowhunting Licenses Sold†	P & Y Bucks Entered†	Ratio
Wisconsin	246,000	469	1 : 524
North Dakota*	11,700	14	1 : 835
Minnesota	66,000	65	1 : 1,015
Oklahoma	21,000	18	1 : 1,166
Ohio	120,000	102	1 : 1,176
Maryland	47,000	40	1 : 1,175
Connecticut	14,000	11	1 : 1,272
Delaware	6,400	5	1 : 1,280
Texas	75,000	58	1 : 1,293
Montana*	26,000	15	1 : 1,733
Missouri	97,417	56	1 : 1,739
Indiana	106,942	52	1 : 2,056
Wyoming*	10,570	5	1 : 2,114
New Jersey	47,575	21	1 : 2,265
New York	170,000	66	1 : 2,575
Kentucky	110,000	40	1 : 2,750
Rhode Island	2,900	1	1 : 2,900
Mississippi	58,000	19	1 : 3,052
Maine	13,000	4	1 : 3,250
New Hampshire	23,580	6	1 : 3,930
Louisiana	33,703	8	1 : 4,212
West Virginia	121,000	28	1 : 4,321
Massachusetts	26,000	6	1 : 4,333
Virginia	58,516	12	1 : 4,876
Michigan	350,000	68	1 : 5,147
Arkansas	30,000	5	1 : 6,000
Georgia	86,000	13	1 : 6,615
Pennsylvania	328,193	41	1 : 8,004
North Carolina	54,000	6	1 : 9,000
Alabama	66,000	7	1 : 9,428
Tennessee	61,000	6	1 : 10,166

State or Province	Bowhunting Licenses Sold[†]	P & Y Bucks Entered[†]	Ratio
Florida	35,000	0	Go for a tan or stay home
Saskatchewan[*]	1,000	10	1 : 100
Alberta[*]	12,200	15	1 : 813

[*]Bowhunting licenses sold in these states or provinces included other species (elk, mule deer, antelope). Because of this, the actual ratios of P & Y whitetails to whitetail hunters are much better than the ratios listed.

[†]Numbers of bowhunting licenses sold taken from *Archery Business* (September–October 2000); P & Y entries taken from *Advantage Whitetail Spectacular* (October 2000).

What this chart shows is that deer that do not experience heavy hunting pressure are much easier to hunt and kill. Why? Not only will deer in these areas behave in a natural fashion that is usually easy to pattern and hunt, but the buck-to-doe ratio will normally be balanced enough to encourage a more competitive rut among bucks, which in turn makes them more susceptible to tactics such as rattling, calling, mock scrapes, and the use of decoys and scents. Most hunting videos are filmed in such settings, if not in fenced enclosures. Strictly from a cost standpoint, videos in which only large, mature bucks are targeted have to be filmed in nonpressured areas, or it would take decades to get enough footage to compare with those already on the market. Average hunting techniques like those presented in most hunting magazines, books, and videos can lead to success in such nonpressured areas but will be far less effective on heavily hunted mature bucks. It is easier to kill big bucks in places with little hunting pressure, even if you are an average hunter. Under what I consider normal circumstances—hunting with competition from hordes of other hunters—most big-name hunters would probably have just as hard a time killing a three-and-a-half-year-old buck as everyone else does.

Because of the difference between hunting pressured and nonpressured deer, a hunter who is unsuccessful in one area may suddenly become very successful in another. I have four acquaintances who live and hunt in various areas in northern Michigan. The cumulative bowhunting experience among these four hunters is well over ninety years, and they have killed three bucks that score over 100 inches in northern Michigan while bowhunting religiously each fall. These guys are all serious bowhunters, and I consider their skill levels to be well above average. In the last five years, each of these hunters has traveled to Illinois, Iowa, or Kansas, all known big-buck states, to bowhunt whitetails.

Randy Williams (above) and Chad Stearns (below), two northern Michigan bowhunters, each with a buck they took while on a trip out of state.

Among the four of them, they have made nine separate one-week out-of-state hunts. During those nine hunts, eight bucks were taken, every one of which scored between 120 and 165 inches. That is a success rate of 89 percent on mature bucks on one-week hunts. Did these hunters suddenly develop better hunting habits while out of state? I don't think so. There simply are more big bucks in the areas they visited, and those bucks are much easier to hunt.

This example is not meant to condemn the hunting in my home state, nor to suggest that you should not hunt in an area with heavy hunting pressure. You should take advantage of the opportunity to bowhunt anywhere you can. Consider yourself lucky if you hunt in an area with little hunting pressure. I just wanted to point out that there are major differences in the number of mature bucks from region to region, and in how easy they are to get close to. It follows that a hunter's skill is not necessarily reflected by the number or quality of bucks he or she has taken. Where you hunt should have a lot to do with your expectations, although location is not everything. To kill mature bucks on a regular basis anywhere is challenging, but it is much more of a challenge where there is heavy hunting pressure.

Magazines and books are full of hunters who are proficient at killing mature bucks in areas with little hunting pressure. Sure, some of them have a good understanding of deer behavior, but their hunting techniques usually will just not work in a hunting situation where there is a lot of pressure and competition. One writer claimed in a recent article that in six seasons he saw more than 130 Pope and Young class bucks. That is more than 20 P & Y bucks per season. This guy is obviously not hunting in a pressured area, where there is no way so many bucks would live to maturity. There is no excuse for this guy not to shoot a couple really big bucks every season. If you see anywhere near that many big bucks in a season, you are not hunting in a pressured area either. While hunting in Michigan, I see on average about three shooter bucks per season, and this number includes repeat sightings of the same buck. For me, a shooter buck is one that will gross score near the P & Y minimum. Score for me is irrelevant, but a buck about that size is usually three and a half years old in my area and is what I try to hunt for. The highest number of bucks I have ever seen in this category in one season was seven in 1997. I did not see any in 1998 or 2002; in 2000 I saw two.

Most hunters in pressured areas see only a few mature bucks per year. Because our hunting situation is so much different than that of the "experts" who hunt nonpressured areas, only a small portion of their hunting methods can be applied in truly pressured areas. Most of these guys have no idea how difficult it is to hunt in areas with heavy hunting pressure.

If you live in an area with heavy hunting pressure and you would like to kill mature bucks, you have a few choices. You can spend your money to hunt in another region or state, you can join a large private hunt club with strictly enforced harvest regulations, you can buy a large tract of property and keep it entirely to yourself, or you can go through the work necessary to refine your hunting technique to be successful on truly pressured mature bucks. Of course, anyone with the money can become a big-dollar big-buck hunter. With enough cash you can buy anything, and that includes trophy bucks. But most of us just do not have the money or the unusual desire necessary for this kind of hunting. This leaves most of us with only one option, and that is to become the best we can with what we are given. Is it impossible to kill big bucks with consistency in heavily hunted areas? Absolutely not! There is, however, a big difference in how you have to hunt to accomplish this.

When hunting pressured mature bucks, you cannot afford to make any mistakes. The scenarios depicted in most videos are not appropriate for hunting in these situations. Sitting as low and exposed in your tree as those hunters do will not work with any consistency, and arriving at your tree just prior to dawn is intolerable. And all the whispering and movement that take place in videos as the big mature buck is approaching could frighten off pressured bucks. My opportunities at mature bucks are so infrequent that I don't even want another human around.

Another reality in most heavy hunted areas is nocturnal bucks—mature bucks that leave sign but are rarely seen during shooting hours. These bucks, as well as the matriarch does, move through the woods as if walking on eggshells, looking into the tree branches for lurking bowhunters. Many of these bucks have paid for their lapses in caution with their own blood. I have taken two bucks from very heavily hunted areas that aged out at over seven years. Both of those bucks had several healed-over wounds from encounters with hunters in previous years. It is obvious that these bucks were on extreme alert and tuned in to any sign of hunting; they knew they were playing for keeps. These hard-hunted mature bucks are fewer in number than their nonpressured brethren, and it is quite possible that a two-and-a-half-year-old here behaves as cautiously as a five-and-a-half-year-old in less pressured areas.

Many hunters claim that there aren't any mature bucks in the areas where they hunt. There may not be many, but I guarantee there are some—or at least one—though they may be rarely seen, and then only fleetingly. This fact has been coming to light in recent years with the increased use of remote, motion-triggered cameras. Every year a lot of hunters are surprised to find out that there are indeed mature bucks living on or using their hunting property. I believe that in most cases, after a buck reaches four years of age in a hard-hunted area, his odds of dying from natural causes or an accident are greater than falling to a hunter. In order to have regular success with these bucks, you have to hunt with more intensity and be more precise, smarter, and better prepared than most other hunters.

CHAPTER 2

Finding Places to Hunt

Sometimes the most difficult aspect of hunting pressured mature white-tails is finding a place to hunt. Like the deer, landowners in heavily hunted areas tend to be hunter-shy. Getting permission to hunt hasn't always been a problem. When I started to bow hunt in the 1960s, it was easy to simply knock on a door and get permission. Back then, the question was apt to be "You want to do what?" And permission was granted with a grin and a chuckle.

Times have changed, and getting permission to hunt seems to get more difficult every year. Urban sprawl is eating up huntable land at an alarming rate. The number of urban antihunters moving to rural areas is also increasing dramatically, and this is closing off land from hunting as well. Often landowners are not necessarily antihunting but are approached regularly for permission to hunt. In some cases, their land is already being hunted. Many have had bad experiences with hunters or other recreational land users destroying their property or just not respecting the fact that they are on someone else's land. Sometimes these landowners just stop allowing hunting all together. Hunters themselves are also placing limits on huntable land. Modern private quality deer management practices and big-money leases for good hunting property are closing a lot of hunters out. The bottom line is that there simply are more hunters competing for diminishing space. Don't expect to knock on a farmer's door in September and receive permission to bowhunt the upcoming season. In heavily hunted areas, the chances of that happening are about as good as those of winning the lottery.

This can be very discouraging, but the good news is that with a little effort, it is possible to find places to hunt even in the hardest-hunted areas. I like to approach the task as if I were looking for a job. Getting a new job can be difficult and time-consuming, and negative responses are part of the game. If you approach asking for permission with this attitude, it will make the entire process easier to handle.

There are a couple different ways to get permission to hunt. The easiest way is by networking. Whether at work, church, school, or anywhere else, let people know you're looking for a place to hunt. As you spread the word around, so will your friends and acquaintances, and you may get permission from an unexpected source—someone's friend or relative who owns property somewhere. The chances of getting permission through networking are better than if you just go knocking on doors, simply because it is more difficult for landowners to turn down a person they know or who is recommended by a family member or friend. Always keep in mind that permission to hunt anywhere is better than no permission at all. Even if the property is no bigger than five acres, it will probably have deer crossing it and could be an awesome, overlooked spot. If hunted properly, several small properties can be as productive as one large area, sometimes even more so.

The other way to obtain permission is by knocking on doors. In heavily hunted areas, this is extremely difficult. Begin by locating areas where you'd like to hunt and finding out who the landowners are. You can do this by looking in county plat books, available from the county clerk's office, which list the owners of the various properties along with the size and shape of each property. Every few years, I buy new plat books for the counties I like to hunt the most. I compare these new books with the old ones. If a property on which I would like to hunt has changed hands, I will ask the new owner for permission. Again, don't let the size of a parcel deter you from checking it out. Small, five- or ten-acre parcels with one or two stand locations that get hunted only two or three times each season can be quite productive. Big is not always better when it comes to hunting property.

Before you go knocking on doors, plan ahead. I have a simple résumé prepared that I give to landowners. It includes my job, general information about my family, years of hunting experience, hunting and conservation groups I belong to, and other hobbies (this can sometimes give you a common subject to talk about). It also states that I will treat the landowner's property with respect, as though it were my own; follow all landowner wishes; leave the property as I found it; and hunt alone. Hunting alone is very important when seeking permission. Landowners are more likely to give you permission if they know you are not going to be bringing in a bunch of people. After you've hunted there for a few years and developed a trusting relationship with the landowner, he or she may be willing to allow you to bring a friend along. If you are serious about pursuing mature bucks, it is best done alone anyway.

Timing is also important. The best time to ask for hunting permission is in late winter or early spring. During this time of year, landowners are not thinking too much about hunting. They may even be caught by surprise at the request and be a little more likely to grant permission. In some instances, the property owner may ask you to come back later in the summer or just prior to hunting season. This is a good sign. When you return, he'll have a more difficult time turning you down, because you did what he asked of you. Believe it or not, acquiring permission can sometimes be a mental game played between hunter and property owner, and you must be willing to play. In the spring, you also might consider offering a farmer a helping hand in some way in exchange for hunting permission. You may not have to help at all, but a farmer will definitely appreciate the offer, and this could go a long way toward developing a sense of trust. The closer it gets to hunting season, the lower your chances of getting permission.

Again as in a job interview, the first impression you make is the most important. Always ask for permission in person. Do not do it over the telephone. It is much more difficult to deny permission face-to-face. Dress casually but nicely. You may think that camouflage is a fashion statement, but most landowners do not. If possible, take your wife with you; it's amazing how much more difficult it is for a property owner to say no to a female. Always talk and act in a very respectful manner, even if you happen to encounter a hardcore antihunter. Being respectful and polite will also help counter the common stereotype that hunters are depraved and twisted barbarians. Remember that image is everything in our fast-paced world, and the future of hunting depends on hunters maintaining a good image. Even if you are denied permission, and this will most likely be the result of most attempts, always thank the landowners for their valuable time and leave your résumé. Now the landowner knows who you are, and if you are polite, there is no rule stating that you cannot ask for permission again. You never know what could happen. Perhaps a hunter who has hunted the property for several years will move or decide to hunt somewhere else. The next attempt could gain you permission. A word of caution: There is a difference between determination and harassment. Do not overdo it. I live across the road from a property owner with a prime ten-acre parcel. I have politely asked him for permission every year for the last twelve years and have not received it yet, but one of these years he may say yes. And with a property owner like that, you know that if you do get permission, you'll have the hunting all to yourself.

Acquiring permission in heavily hunted areas is just as important as scouting. In pressured areas with major property fragmentation, you must have several places to hunt to be consistently successful. Hunting rights are lost when property is sold or developed, and permission is a part of the game that you must keep on top of. It seems like every year I lose one or two pieces of hunting property, and those must be replaced with other properties. After you receive permission to hunt, take care that you do not lose that permission. Keep a friendly and polite relationship with the landowner. Report anything out of the usual that you see on the property. Follow any rules you are given. Some farmers request that you harvest does as well as bucks. Make sure you do this. If you do kill a deer on the property, always offer some meat to the landowner. A Christmas card that includes a brief thank-you for the hunting permission, or even a small gift to show your gratitude, can do wonders. Not only is property expensive to purchase, but there also are taxes to be paid. Do not take permission to hunt for granted; it can be taken away as fast as it was given.

CHAPTER 3

Scouting and Preparation

Preparation is the key to successfully hunting mature pressured bucks. The more prepared you are, the better your chances of killing mature bucks on a regular basis. Once the preparation is completed, hunting is the easy part, provided you do so carefully and with a plan. Scouting thoroughly and correctly, as part of meticulous preparation, can mean the difference between success and failure. When and how you scout are vital to consistent success.

POSTSEASON (DECEMBER–APRIL)

Most of your scouting and stand preparation should be done between December and the end of April. The work you do at this time of year should encompass 80 percent of the physical work you do throughout the hunting year, hunting included. If you want to kill mature bucks in heavily hunted areas, you need to scout and prepare your stands postseason, or immediately after the snow is gone. Snow causes deer to seek out the most easily accessible food sources and travel routes. Therefore, sign left in snow is a poor indicator of fall deer movement. For safety reasons, don't begin your postseason scouting until gun season is over.

Why would you do most of your scouting at this time, knowing the sign you are reading could be from a buck that was killed during gun season or is no longer in the area? The buck that made the sign might indeed not be around anymore, but if the property is such that it attracted one dominant or mature buck, it should attract another. This may not happen until the prerut the following season, but if the area holds does, bucks will eventually show up.

Also, any sign you encounter at this time of year was made during hunting season. This is much more valuable information than the sign deer leave in the summer, because summer deer movement is completely different from fall deer movement. Most importantly, there will still be sign from the rut phases. This sign can clue you in to how the deer react to hunting pressure and allow you to prepare for it. The best thing about postseason scouting, though, is that you can investigate every inch of the property on which you hunt without having to worry about leaving scent or spooking deer. And with the woods as barren as they are in the winter, it's easier to get a feel for the property without having to bushwhack, as you might have to do in the summer. When I scout a property in the winter, I leave no stone unturned, thoroughly checking every part of the property to get a feel for how and why the deer move as they do.

Don't worry about spooking deer while scouting at this time of year. Spooking deer may indicate nonpressured areas you overlooked in the past or an escape route you never noticed. If you do spook a deer, watch it carefully and note where it goes. These locations could be hot spots for late next season or when hunting pressure is excessive. If you are scouting after gun season and are jumping deer, it's because they feel safe in these areas. Knowing areas where deer feel safe at this time is useful information for future late-season bowhunting.

When you scout a property for the first time, the first thing to do is walk the perimeter. Carrying a notebook, begin to map the obvious features such as ridges, saddles, swales, ditches, apple and oak trees, cropfields, and bedding areas. Then return to the best perimeter sign and follow it to the interior of the property. As you go, add detail to your map. Continue this process by following all perimeter sign into the interior until all the features of the property are mapped out. Never assume an area with cover is too small to hold deer until you check it out. Some of the best bucks I've taken in the past ten years have come from small areas I would not have even looked at twenty years ago. One of the biggest bucks I've ever seen jumped out of a tiny swale not much bigger than a large brush pile, along a fencerow running through the middle of a huge alfalfa field. Unfortunately, I was rabbit hunting after gun season.

After covering nearly every inch of the property, you'll have a good idea where the deer move on the property and why. Pay attention to sign across the perimeter on the neighboring properties as well. It's a good idea to try to get a clear indication of where, when, and why deer are entering or leaving the property.

Only after you have inspected the entire area should you begin to think about preparing trees. Unlike fall scouting, when you should spend as little time as possible in the area so as not to spook deer, at this time of year there is no need to hurry. You can take several weeks to fully investigate and set up the property. You simply cannot do that in the fall without drastically hurting your chances of taking a mature buck. Take your time, enjoy being out in the woods, and do the work necessary to be successful at hunting mature pressured bucks.

Preparing stand locations properly is critical to their success. Always pick the tree that is closest to the most activity but still offers cover, not the one that appears to be easier to set up. When choosing a tree, consider how much cover the tree will offer you at the time you will be hunting there. During the early part of the season all the trees will have plenty of leaves to offer good cover. However, by the time the rut phases come, most of the tree foliage and brush foliage will be gone, offering you nothing but the tree itself for cover. Knowing that you will not be hunting a location until that period should help to determine the tree you pick. Try to find a tree with a large-diameter crotch to give you some cover. You may be hunting in the best location available, but if the tree you're in doesn't offer cover, the likelihood of getting a shot off with the foliage gone diminishes drastically. Also, when preparing trees you will hunt when the foliage is gone, set your stand a little bit higher to help keep you out of the deer's peripheral vision. This will allow you to get away with some slight movements, but still try to set a stand so as little body movement as possible is needed to shoot at the majority of the sign.

Once you choose the best tree for a stand, you must consider how frequently you'll use it. Many hunters hunt the same two or three stands during the entire season, either because of limited property access, or simply because it requires less preparation. If you plan on hunting from a small number of trees, you should prepare stand locations on very defined travel routes or at specific destination points, where as little cover as possible has to be removed in order to get a shot off. The lanes you cut should be fairly narrow, and the trees you're in should have just enough branches cut out to offer a clean shot while leaving you as much cover as possible. It doesn't take many encounters with a hunter in a stand for a mature doe to notice the intrusion, either by sight, sound, or smell, and the more open the area is where you hunt, the more quickly you will get picked off. If you have multiple locations and don't hunt any of them more than five times in a season—which is definitely a huge advantage from a surprise standpoint—then you should cut wider lanes, and trim the tree you're hunting in for more shot opportunities. Trees set up for the prerut and rut periods must have wide, totally cleared out lanes for several possible shot locations, because deer can come from any direction then, totally disregarding any patterns or sign, and mature bucks may pursue a doe through areas they'll never revisit.

Every piece of property you scout will be different, with its own unique elements. Most features and sign that you locate will remain

Trees with multiple scrapes under them are considered primary scrape areas that get revisited.

constant year after year. Bedding areas, funnels, primary scrape areas, food sources, and water holes usually stay the same from one season to the next. Over the years, I have developed a sort of hierarchy of the types of sign or cover I consider to be the most important to look for on a piece of land.

Primary Scrape Areas

The first thing to look for is primary scrape areas. They are sometimes difficult to find, but if there are a bedding area and a feeding area on a property, there should be at least one primary scrape area as well. Look for several scrapes in a small area with overhanging licking branches above them (discussed further in chapter 9). A licking branch or overhead limb will have been nipped off and chewed on, and there is usually more than one over each scrape. These branches are scent-marked by mature deer in the area by rubbing them with the preorbital glands at the corner of the eye, and licking or nipping them. Although licking branches are used primarily by bucks, mature does will use them as well. Scrape areas are not yet entirely understood, but we do know that they relay a host of information to all deer in the herd. Licking branches over some primary scrapes are used all year round for social reasons. The dominant buck and other bucks in an area will visit primary scrape areas.

Some places to look for primary scrape areas are in funnels between bedding areas, funnels between bedding and feeding areas, around apple trees, on small oak ridges, at the tips of wooded or brushy fingers protruding into cropfields, at corners of cropfields, and at bases of ridges that drop off into marshy areas or swamps. Primary scrape areas found along edges of crops (other than standing corn), by fencerows with sparse cover, or at an individual tree in an open area will rarely be visited during daylight hours in pressured areas and usually are not worth hunting.

When you find a primary scrape area, treat it as though it were precious. They are relatively rare, hard to find, and should be real hot spots if hunted properly. When you clear out a tree in a primary scrape area, set up in a location from which you can cover as much of the area as possible. Because this area will be hunted only a few times during a short period, you must have enough shooting lanes cut to be able to shoot at anything entering the area. These scrape areas are usually small, twenty to thirty yards in diameter, but I have seen some that were up to eighty yards long and had as many as fifteen scrapes. In those instances, you must set up in the core, if possible, so that all the edges are within range. There is no guarantee that a buck will pass through the middle of a primary scrape area. He may very well work one of the perimeter scrapes and move on,

These scrapes found during season were only two of the nine scrapes in the immediate area, a primary scrape area.

or just skirt the downwind edge and scent-check the area. Your stand location should allow you a shot in such a circumstance.

Winter and early spring are the time to set up your stands and clear out your trees in primary scrape areas for the upcoming season. Take your time as you clear shooting lanes, place your climbing steps, mark the route to your tree with reflective tacks so you will be able to find it in the dark on morning hunts, and make certain everything is perfect. Marking your entry is very important during winter and early-spring scouting. The woods will look entirely different once the foliage returns, and on morning hunts, you may wander around in the dark trying to find your tree if the trail is not marked. I like to use green reflective tacks because they are more difficult for other hunters to see in the daytime.

Stands in primary scrape areas should be your best bet for killing a mature buck, so pay attention to detail. You might also consider preparing two trees, if possible, in the same spot for different wind conditions. After you have completed preparing your trees, stay away from the spot. This will ensure that there will not be an excessive amount of human odor in the area prior to season and will allow the deer, especially the mature bucks, to follow their natural routine undisturbed.

Primary scrape areas are my top priority because they have been my most productive hunting locations for dominant bucks. These areas are perennial unless there is a severe change in habitat such as occur due to

Mature bucks feel more comfortable moving through funnels of brush between two open fields, such as the one pictured here (marked with an X).

crop rotation, logging, or property development. A stand in an active primary scrape area should be one of your best when hunted properly.

Funnels Between Bedding Areas

The second thing to look for while scouting are funnels between bedding areas (described below). These funnels may consist of any of several terrain types: a wide overgrown fencerow, narrow patch of brush, weedy ditch, low area of thick brush between two large thickets—basically anywhere there is condensed cover. A funnel can even be as simple as a couple trees connecting two areas of cover. A spot I hunted in the late seventies consisted of a single oak tree between the corner of a large patch of white pines and a large area of hardwoods. On the other two sides were open fields of short weeds that did not provide any cover. There was no evidence of buck activity anywhere near this tree. The reason for this was obvious: There were no small trees or bushes suitable to leave sign on. The deer in this area were feeding in the larger weed field at night, and then moving into the pines at daylight. They took their time dispersing from the pines to the hardwoods nearby to feed on acorns and bed down. The pines were mature and did not offer any good ground cover in which to bed. The single oak was the only tree, and thus provided the only available cover, between the pines and the hardwoods. I took an eight-point and an eleven-point buck from that tree. When faced with the choice of crossing an open field or taking a route with cover, even very little cover, deer will almost always choose the route with cover. When you find a funnel like this, try to set up in a tree that will provide you with good cover.

As with primary scrape areas, you should clear out trees in these areas in the winter. The idea is the same. Get your stands in place now so you will not alert deer to your presence just prior to season. Funnels between bedding areas have to be hunted almost the same way as primary scrape areas. Hunt the spot very sparingly until the prerut starts, at which time these areas will begin to receive a lot of attention from mature dominant bucks, especially during midday, as they cruise from bedding area to bedding area scent-checking for estrous does. Therefore, during the prerut, it's important to hunt these spots until at least 2 P.M., or if you have the time, all day.

When you clear out a tree in a funnel, make sure you can shoot the entire width of the funnel, or at least as much of it as possible. Choose the spot where the funnel is narrowest and the runways or sign most concentrated. If there is a runway out of range of your tree, move branches or brush around in order to make the deer come closer. Deer will not walk through piled brush unless they absolutely have to. Perhaps there is a deadfall or a fallen treetop in the area, or just some branches lying around. Stack this material in such a manner that deer using that runway will be funneled closer to you. This is best done in the winter. If you get the deer moving the way you want in the winter, it will be habit by the time hunting season rolls around.

Funnels Between Bedding and Feeding Areas

Funnels between bedding and feeding areas are always a good bet and should be the next area of concentration on your winter scouting tour. Prepare your trees as described for funnels between two bedding areas. Make sure everything is perfect. This is a location where anything can happen at any time, which means you can hunt these funnels throughout the season. I have many such trees that I hunt during the slow weeks in mid-October. You'll probably see numerous does. This can be either positive or negative, depending on the situation. Does will attract mature bucks during the prerut and rut. On the other hand, you have to be very careful not to spook does while in or going to and from your stand. If you spook them, they will avoid the funnel, and this could be enough to alert a mature buck to your presence, causing him to avoid the area as well.

Rub Lines

After you have covered all the funnels on the property, look for rub lines (discussed further in chapter 11). Rub lines of mature bucks will generally have a pattern. Even though it is winter and you will be looking at the previous season's rubs, you should set up a stand where there is any pattern of large rubs. If the buck that made the rubs is still alive, he will more than likely follow the same pattern as he did the previous year. If that buck did not survive, there's a good chance that whatever caused him to use that particular route will attract another mature buck.

Saddles and Ridges

Also keep your eyes open for saddles and ridges. A saddle is a low area bordered closely by hills or ridges on both sides. These terrain features are more prevalent in regions where there are mountains and large areas of big hills. Saddles usually offer deer cover and easy passage from area to area without having to climb hills or walk over uneven ground. They also give deer an advantage with the wind currents.

While these low passageways are usually well traveled, they frustrated me for years. They were difficult to hunt because the constantly

A rub line found in early spring should be checked prior to the following season, at which time it will make a good early ambush site if it is still active.

changing wind direction, due to morning and afternoon thermals, made it extremely difficult to conceal my scent from the deer. In the morning, as the temperature is rising, the wind currents, known as thermals, are also rising. As the temperature starts to fall in the late afternoon, the wind currents fall as well. At the bottom of a saddle or ridge, these wind currents meet and swirl in every direction. I stopped hunting saddles and bases or sides of ridges about fifteen years ago and only started hunting them again after I began using an activated carbon Scent-Lok suit (discussed further in chapter 5) to conceal my scent from the deer. If there is a defined saddle on your property connecting high-traffic areas, and if you plan to wear an activated carbon suit and practice diligent scent control, place a stand at the narrowest point in the bottom of the saddle.

Feeding Areas

Always keep your eyes open for mast- or fruit-bearing trees hidden from open areas. These attract deer at all times of the season, and they will visit these trees as a first destination after leaving their bedding areas in the evening or just before returning to them in the morning. Apples, acorns, nuts, and chokecherries are the main food sources for deer when available. In years when these trees produce good quantities of fruit or mast, they are about as good as it gets for hunting the early part of the season through late October. For mature bucks to visit them during daylight hours, however, they must be located in adequate cover. Unless you are hunting in an area with an abundance of these trees, the deer have to compete for their fruits. This creates a situation where the deer get to feed on a first-come, first-served basis. Take advantage of fruit- or mast-bearing trees early in the season. Most of these trees are bare by the time the rut periods roll around and will have lost their attraction. Set up on the downwind side within comfortable shooting distance.

Crop rotations are another aspect of your winter scouting. They will affect the way deer move and how you hunt them, so it's a good idea to pay attention to them and learn what crops will be where during the next growing season. Farmers often follow a fairly regular rotation, and after a couple years, the pattern should become obvious. If you know the crop will be corn in the fall, place a couple stands around the perimeter of the field. You can enter and exit a stand along the edge of a standing cornfield without being detected. Stands around fields of short crops, such as picked corn, soybeans, alfalfa, or wheat stubble, should be placed at least twenty yards inside an adjacent woods or within comfortable shooting distance from the edge. This will allow you to get to and leave your stand with less probability of being detected before daylight and after dark, when deer may be feeding in the fields. From your stand inside the woods, you should have a shooting lane cleared to the edge of the field. Mature bucks sometimes walk field edges or, more likely, just inside the woods, scent-checking for estrous does that may have previously entered or exited the field. The deer will use the same runways year after year despite crop rotation, although the amount of use will increase dramatically when the field is planted in corn, due to the daytime security such fields provide.

Also take note of any large oak in a marsh, standing cornfield, swale, or any other bedding area. When these trees have acorns, they will attract deer, and even more so than usual because they are located in bedding areas. These trees are superb spots that a lot of hunters overlook. Imagine how secure a mature buck must feel to get up and feed on acorns while still in the safety of his bedding area. If you sneak into one of these trees quietly, there is always the chance that a mature buck will come in to feed before leaving the security of his bedding area after dark or prior to bedding down for the day.

Additional Travel Corridors

After your stands have been placed in all these major areas, it's time to search out the often-overlooked subtle sign for stand locations. Overlooked travel corridors such as weed-filled ditches or old brushy fencerows, crossing points at low spots in fencerows, holes in fences, and brush along highways can be tremendous ambush locations. Where there is heavy hunting pressure, mature bucks will almost always follow a route with the best available cover or least amount of pressure. If a deep, weed-filled ditch runs past a huntable tree, it should be checked for sign. Deer can travel down a deep ditch without being seen, and if there is no hunting pressure, deer will use this travel corridor all season. In many instances, a ditch will pass by a wooded area and then go through open areas surrounded by crops. When stands are placed along the open areas, entering them undetected is relatively easy on evening hunts. The tree, however, must be large enough to provide background cover; otherwise your silhouette will be easily spotted by passing deer.

Crossing points in fences are also commonly overlooked. In their daily routine, mature deer conserve as much energy as possible and will sometimes alter their route to avoid jumping over a fence. Any spot where there is a hole in a fence or a downed section of fence should be investigated. If there are several openings in a section of fence, clear out a tree at the opening best suited to hunt, and then prop up or fix the fence in the other locations or pile brush in the way. Instead of having many

Low spots or large gaps in and under fences should be major crossing areas.

crossing points to choose from, the deer will now funnel past your tree. This may seem like extra work at the time, but by creating this tighter funnel, you are increasing your chances at taking a mature buck. You should also have a stand near any opening in a fence, such as a gate, where deer pass through regularly, assuming there is adequate cover for daytime use.

Water Holes

Another spot often overlooked by hunters is water holes. During dry years, water holes receive a lot of deer activity and are great ambush sites. Hunting near water holes is especially effective when there is not a lot of other available water in the immediate area. To expect to see deer in the daytime at a water hole, you have to find one with a fair amount of cover. Place a stand on either side of the water hole for varying wind directions. This spot will probably become a staging area (discussed further in chapter 10) once the prerut starts, if the rest of the area is dry, and could turn into a primary scrape area if there is heavy doe activity.

When you hunt water holes in the morning, arrive at your tree at least an hour and a half before daybreak. This is important because mature bucks often stop for a quick drink just before daylight before bedding down, and you do not want to spook them with your entry. You will have

Chris took this ten-point near a waterhole in Montana in September 2001.

Even a small water hole in a relatively dry area can receive a lot of traffic.

the best results hunting water holes after several days of hot, dry weather. During hot, dry spells, deer will also visit water holes regularly during midday, no matter what time of season it is. This can be an excellent opportunity. While hunting state land in Montana on September 2, 2001, Chris killed a beautiful ten-point by setting up at noon next to a water hole on an unseasonably warm day, when the temperature hit 95 degrees. From 2:00 P.M. until dark, there was a constant flow of deer to the water hole. Most of the deer movement was at about 4:00 P.M., just after the hottest part of the day. At one point, two shooter bucks came in and bedded within forty yards. The ten-point bedded for several hours next to the water hole before getting up and presenting Chris with a twenty-five-yard shot, which he made good on. When conditions are right to hunt water holes, it's a good idea to adjust your hunting plans accordingly.

Bedding Areas

While postseason scouting, thoroughly explore any cattail marsh, swamp, or large weed field. These are all bedding areas that can have a great deal of deer activity, and you should know where and when the deer use these areas. The first thing to check for in marshes or swamps is water. The amount of rainfall in the summer will have a large impact on the amount

Marshes or tall weed fields are excellent bedding areas that can be ambushed from groups of trees (often primary scrape areas) protruding into the field.

of deer activity in these areas in the fall. During dry years, all of these areas, especially cattail marshes, will hold more deer than during wet years. The year 1999 was very dry in Michigan, and almost every cattail marsh I entered that year had a virtual maze of runways and was dotted with beds. During most years, these same marshes have far more water in them and far less deer activity. It's important to explore and know the interior makeup of the marshes and swamps on the property you hunt. You can only accomplish this in the winter or early spring without harming your hunting during the season.

If you have a cattail marsh on the property, it can be an excellent place to hunt. The beds you find in dry cattail marshes will look so comfortable that you may be tempted to lie down and take a nap yourself. The maze of runways will funnel into several main exit routes. When I hunt cattail marshes, I like to hunt these exit routes as close to the exit as possible while still within the marsh. After you decide on an exit route you want to hunt, prepare your visual and shooting lanes on the side of the route that best suits the predominant wind direction. About ten yards to the side of the exit route, clear out a three- to four-foot area. Remove everything down to the bare dirt so that your movements will remain completely silent. Stomp down two lanes about eighteen inches wide each from this spot back to the exit route. The two lanes should look like a V in the cattails. The open ends of the V should be about five yards apart on the deer's exit route. One of your lanes is a visual lane and the other is a shooting lane, depending on which way the deer is traveling. The way you use these lanes is to draw your bow when the deer you're after passes the visual lane, and shoot when he enters the shooting lane.

Try to place as much cover between you and the deer as possible to keep from being spotted. In a cattail marsh, you can do this by setting up broken cattails in front of you. Be creative. Deer have amazing peripheral vision, so when you're going to be hunting on the ground, you need plenty of cover.

When you hunt on the ground in a field or marsh, it's important to wear very light beige camouflage to match the surroundings. If you wear your normal tree stand camouflage, you'll be very conspicuous and will probably be spotted by the first deer that crosses your visual lane. Try not to touch any plants while approaching your spot, and wear an activated carbon suit as an undergarment.

Observation Stands
Also consider building one or more observation stands. These stands should be far from where you will be hunting, perhaps in a tree across the

Aerial surveys give a unique perspective on the land you hunt.

field from where deer enter and exit or along an out-of-the-way fencerow. They have to be far enough away from the areas used by the deer that you won't risk spooking them. You also must be able to approach and depart your observation points undetected.

Putting It All Together

After you've prepared all your trees and hunting lanes, complete your map by placing all of these locations on it, along with any new information you have discovered. Note the types of trees you have selected. Each tree species loses its leaves at a different time. This can be valuable information when you are establishing a hunting plan for a particular area late in the fall, when most of the foliage is down.

If it's still not clear to you why deer move through your property as they do, there are other resources that can be very informative. Topographical maps and photographs, combined with your map and scouting experience, can provide you with insight into how and why the deer move the way they do over your hunting property. These resources can also help you get the big picture of your property in relation to the neighboring properties.

If maps and topographical photos do not provide the information you had hoped for, you can take your own aerial photos. I like to do this when I have several small parcels to hunt within a fifty-mile radius of each other. Plane rides cost between $100 and $200 per hour in my area, and you might even find a pilot who has some experience with photographers. You should take your flight on a calm, clear late-fall or winter day, when the canopy of leaves is gone. This will give you an overall picture of what the property looks like and how dense the cover really is, because you will be able to see what is below the treetops. You can also see any funnels or terrain features on bordering properties that will naturally cause deer traffic to flow to certain areas on your property. Several pieces of property can be easily visited in an hour, so take a friend and split the cost. It is absolutely amazing how funnels, points, fingers, ridges, bedding areas, and other areas utilized by deer simply jump out at you when seen from the air. This could be some of the quickest, most effective scouting you ever do.

LATE SPRING–EARLY SUMMER (MAY–JULY)
In May through July, with your trees prepared and shooting lanes cleared out, your emphasis should shift to more general scouting. This means that while you're enjoying the summer with your family and friends, always keep your eyes and ears open for new property to hunt. When you see a place that looks good, note the location and stop sometime later to ask for permission. If a landowner grants you permission in the late spring or early summer, you still have time to scout the property and prepare your hunting sites without disturbing the deer movement for the upcoming fall.

During this time of year, you should also pay a visit to all the landowners from whom you already have permission. Confirm your permission to hunt on their land during the coming season, and let them know how much you appreciate their allowing you to do so. A short visit can mean the difference between having a place to hunt another year or having to look elsewhere.

PRESEASON (AUGUST–SEPTEMBER)
This is the time of year hunters typically begin scouting for the upcoming season, and by doing so, they often ruin their chances at arrowing a mature buck. There are several things that make preseason scouting during August and September problematic. Mature bucks react severely to human presence, and after being left alone all summer, they notice the sudden influx of human activity. Because of the warm weather, most people tend to scout in the early morning or evening, which are the times when deer are also moving the most, making matters even worse. This

will cause mature bucks to either move to an undisturbed area or enter a more nocturnal routine. By scouting at this time, you are giving the adult deer an early warning of the approaching season.

Another problem with scouting at this time is that the deer are in a summer routine, which is a relatively poor indicator of how they will be moving later during the rut periods, when your chances of killing a mature buck are the greatest. Deer movement patterns often change dramatically throughout the course of the season. There is not much you can learn about the late-fall movement of deer in the late summer. Either most of your stand locations will be set up in position to intercept summer movement patterns, which is fine only for the first few days of season, or you'll simply be guessing what the deer will be doing later in the season. This is why the best scouting is done postseason, when you are following sign made during the rut.

The thick brush and foliage at this time of year also make scouting more difficult. Not only does it obscure the subtle details of the land, but it also makes it harder to traverse the entire property, prepare your trees, and clear hunting lanes. The lanes also will be far more obvious to the deer than if they had been prepared in the winter, and leaving human scent is nearly unavoidable when dragging branches and small trees away from the hunting location at this time of year.

Still, there are a few things you need to do at this time. In late August or early September, it's a good idea to make a quick tour of your existing stands and hunting lanes to make final touch-ups before the season. When you do this, it is imperative that you remain as undetected as possible. Pull on your activated carbon suit, rubber boots, and head cover, and sneak as silently as you can to each hunting site. Remove all new growth from your shooting lanes. You might also have to place tree steps or hang a stand. Whatever you do, do not linger or do any new scouting. The faster you leave the area and the less scent you leave behind, the better.

Once you've made sure all your stands and shooting lanes are ready for the season, do not revisit them until it's time to hunt. Concentrate your hunting to the transition zones from bedding to feeding areas and the actual feeding areas during the early part of the season. Save the prerut and rut locations until late October in the midwestern and northern states. You want to keep the area clear of human scent until the prerut, when mature bucks start coming out of their nocturnal mid-October patterns. If you hunt your prerut and rut locations prior to this time you will be leaving scent and perhaps spooking does or subordinate bucks. Once you spook does in these hot locations, because of overhunting, the odds of having an encounter with a mature buck diminish drastically.

Revisit your rub line stands during midday in mid to late September, and be on the lookout for new rubs. Don't go out of the way to do this, but if you notice one, definitely check it out. Mature bucks started rubbing their antlers in early September, and will be rubbed out by this time. If you notice a well-used rub line, prepare a tree along its route. Assuming the area has not been disturbed by preseason scouting or other human activity, most bucks will have a fairly consistent movement pattern that early in the season and will follow their rub lines. A rub line is a decent place to hunt throughout the season, as it indicates a buck's regular travel route. If you are careful not to place too much hunting pressure on a rub line, your chances are fair every time you hunt along one. In many heavily hunted areas, however, you must hunt a mature buck during the first few days of season if you are to have any chance of intercepting him following his summer routine.

Now is a good time to try to locate a mature buck to shoot during the first couple days of the season. If you can pattern a mature buck just before the season, your chances of a shot opportunity within the first couple days are pretty good. In order to do this without spooking the buck, you have to keep your distance. If you have set up an observation stand when you set up your stands in the winter, this will make it easier. Wear an activated carbon suit while sitting in the stand. Only if you can spot a mature buck without allowing him to detect you will you be able to get a bead on him while he is still in his summer routine. If you spook a mature buck in a pressured area, the game could very well be over. It might also be possible to do your long-distance scouting from a car. By cruising roads past the fields you hunt, you might see a buck during his daily routine.

When you figure out the pattern of a mature buck, stay out of the area until the first few days of season. The last thing you want to do is alarm this deer. Then either hunt an existing stand or quietly set up a new spot along his route on opening day. If unsuccessful after a couple hunts, leave the area and revert to your normal tactics.

IN-SEASON SCOUTING FOR THE PRERUT AND RUT

Keep any scouting during season to an absolute minimum. Every time you go in and out of your hunting area without taking the buck you are after, your odds of taking him diminish. If for some reason you are not happy about your prepared hunting locations, sometimes scouting for new locations during the season is your only alternative. The reasons for doing this vary, but I usually scout during the season only if the buck sign I expected to show up does not materialize. Bowhunting has many unforeseen variables, and sometimes, despite thorough postseason scouting, things just do not happen as planned. Perhaps another hunter moved in too close to your spot, causing the deer to alter their pattern, or the crop situation is completely different than expected, or some human activity has altered the deer's movement from a travel corridor. Whatever the situation, it is time to act. Sometimes this can mean just a small adjustment of a few hundred yards; other times, you might even have to abandon a property. While hunting, you have to be prepared to adjust.

A good example of in-season scouting and adjustment during the prerut occurred during a three-day hunt Chris was on during the last week of October 1993 in southern Michigan. He was hunting a long finger of woods that jutted far into a huge cornfield. While hunting one evening and the following morning in crisp, cold weather, he had not seen a deer. He thought this was strange for several reasons. The weather was perfect. The area had a relatively high deer population, and he was hunting a primary scrape area that was one of the main crossing points for deer in that section. And two weeks earlier he had hunted this spot and seen numerous deer, including several small bucks, and he had not set foot on the property since. The total lack of deer activity indicated that something was just not right.

After his morning hunt, Chris decided to investigate. Sneaking along the edge of the woods, he soon discovered what had changed the deer's pattern. About sixty yards from his tree, another hunter had set up a tenfoot-tall ladder stand. Ten yards in front of the stand was a pile of apples. Upon inspection of the stand, Chris found numerous cigarette butts, indicating that someone had hunted there quite recently. This hunter had completely altered the normal deer movement through the usually heavily traveled funnel.

Chris continued searching carefully to learn what the deer had done in reaction to the pressure, and about three hundred yards from his original spot, in a small woods, he found what he was looking for. Or, rather, he smelled what he was looking for. He could smell the scent of a buck in full rut, and he walked just far enough in the woods to see a fresh scrape under an apple tree. Numerous new rubs were also in sight. Chris mentally marked a tree within shooting distance of the scrape and quietly left the scene.

He returned at 2:00 P.M. and, after shaking some apples out of the tree, set up in his Ambush Sling a mere fifteen yards away. At 5:00 P.M., a doe came in to feed on the apples. After a few minutes, she became very nervous and slowly walked away. Chris knew what that meant and anxiously waited for the situation to develop. He did not have to wait long. After only a couple minutes, a ten-point came into view and moved toward the

After reacting to another hunter during the season, Chris took this ten-point.

apple tree, quartering away at a distance of only nine yards. Chris took the shot and ended a very rewarding hunt. This was Chris's biggest buck at that time, and one he never would have taken if he had not done a little scouting and adjusted to the situation. It was clear that the ladder stand hunter had unwittingly forced the deer to move their center of activity.

If you decide that it's absolutely necessary to fully scout the property during the season, there are a few times when it's best to do this. Whenever possible, wait for inclement weather to scout. During or immediately after a rainstorm or in strong winds, your likelihood of being detected is reduced. Deer do not move much during heavy rains and high winds, and the noise you make while trimming lanes and trees will more than likely go undetected. Your human odor also will not linger in the area as it would if you scouted on a nice, calm day. Scouting after a heavy rain is not as good as the other two conditions, because the wet ground will hold scent, but it will at least mask most of the noise you make as you move through the area.

When preparing trees during bad weather, make sure you wear a climbing safety belt when preparing a stand location, as trees can be very slippery when wet. Also wear an activated carbon suit and rubber boots so that you leave as little human odor as possible in your hunting area. An item that saves a lot of time is an extendable tree-trimming saw with a rope and pulley branch cutter. You can cut branches twenty feet off the ground with these trimmers. Extendable saws can be purchased at any hardware store and some sporting goods stores.

If you do scout during season, look for a primary scrape area, staging area, major rub line, funnel between two bedding areas, or activity at inside corners of picked cropfields. These are found in high-traffic areas and should be hunted only if they offer surrounding cover. These types of locations will give you the best odds of shooting a mature buck during the prerut and rut.

If you are fortunate enough to find an active primary scrape area or staging area to hunt, you are indeed in luck. These areas are not frequent sights, but when found, they are true hot spots while active, if hunted properly. At a primary scrape area, you have about a five- to ten-day window of exceptional opportunity for killing the dominant buck in the area. Once the full-blown rut starts, this area will still receive a lot of activity, but there's a good chance the buck you are pursuing will be chasing does full-time and will not need to use his scrape area. Hunting over an active primary scrape or staging area is the only time I will hunt a single spot frequently, and I make it a point to stay on stand during midday. Subordinate bucks will also frequent these scrape areas, so don't assume that if a buck comes by, he is the only one using it. Scrapes along open field edges are usually frequented only during the security of darkness in pressured areas.

Any good sign coming in or out of a bedding area, such as rub lines, should be hunted as close to the bedding area as possible without spooking deer in the bedding area with your arrival and setup noise on evening hunts. By this time of the season, there should be an occasional scrape along the rub line if the buck is a mature one. A bedding area is to deer like your house is to you. There are only so many doors in or out, but unlimited directions to go once you get outside. This means that the closer you are to a deer's normal entry or exit trail, the better your chances of killing that deer.

Funnels between bedding areas are awesome during the prerut. Mature bucks will bed prior to daylight and get up after most of the deer traffic has passed through, and then scent-check the perimeters of the bedding areas for estrous does. This movement by mature bucks is generally done between 9:30 A.M. and 2:00 P.M. If nothing catches a buck's interest in one bedding area, he will move on to the next one within his core area. Mature bucks almost always use the best available cover when traveling from one area to the next. This is why a funnel of good cover is your best bet for an ambush.

Bucks going from one point to another with an open picked cropfield in between will skirt the inside, wooded corner of the field. The reason is simple. This is the shortest route without exposing himself in the open. Your stand location should be fifteen to twenty yards inside the corner, with a lane cleared out that will enable you to shoot to the corner. If none of the signs mentioned exist on your property, try to find the location where the most runways converge, and place a stand about fifteen yards away from the intersection. Any stands from which you have been regularly seeing mature does within shooting distance should remain in place and be hunted every few days.

When you find the sign you are looking for, set your stands within easy shooting distance, ten to twenty yards, of your prospective shot opportunity. Never set up directly over your anticipated shot location. This not only gives you a bad shooting angle, but also puts you directly in a deer's line of vision as it is moving toward you, making it very difficult to get away with any movements. When you set up a spot on hot sign during the prerut or rut, you should hunt it for a day or two, back off for a couple days, and then return. At this time of year, you can get away with hunting a spot a couple days in a row, but do not overdo it.

LOCATING BUCKS AFTER GUN SEASON

Gun season has a dramatic effect on deer movement in most parts of the country. Locating mature bucks can and will be a problem during this time of year. If you were thorough during your postseason scouting in previous years, you should know of some areas where deer feel comfortable bedding after gun season. If not, you have your work cut out for you. Mature bucks are so in tune to their surroundings after gun season that spooking them while scouting will more than likely ruin any potential opportunity in that location. Mark any potential stand locations in or near bedding areas where deer are spooked during postseason scouting trips, and have stands set in them before the next season so that they are ready to hunt after gun season.

In areas that have a lot of gun hunting pressure, there will be 60 to 80 percent fewer bucks left alive, and the ones that do remain (even the one-and-a-half-year-olds by now) are usually back to their nocturnal habits. Scouting at this time near bedding areas will only make matters worse. On top of that, even the does seem to become nocturnal in hard-hunted areas. The longer you wait to hunt after gun season, the better your chances of connecting with a mature buck. In northern states, snow and cold weather force all deer to feed more aggressively. The mature breeding bucks need to replenish the weight they lost chasing does during the rut.

Scouting for well-traveled transition routes at this time is your best bet. Travel routes between feeding and bedding areas become very defined, due to the lack of cover in the woods. With the onset of winter, deer start to congregate in groups, making their movements much easier to pinpoint. There is always a chance that an unbred doe or early-born doe fawn will come into estrus during this period and have a good buck pursuing her. These routes are your best odds of taking a buck after gun season.

CHAPTER 4

Using an Ambush Hunting Sling

The weather was perfect and the deer should have been moving, but for a few days I had seen next to nothing. After a beautiful and cold late-October morning without sighting any deer, I knew something was wrong, so I decided to take a quick look around the property. What I found was not a surprise. The deer had simply changed their pattern to avoid the bowhunters, perhaps myself included. Within a couple hundred yards, I found two very fresh scrapes. The larger one was at least three feet across. The buck I was pursuing had changed his travel pattern, and it was time to adjust.

In a matter of minutes, I had a tree ready to go within shooting distance of the scrapes. That afternoon, I was there and anticipated success. In many situations, and this was definitely one of them, the first time a stand is hunted is the best. A while later, I noticed a deer moving up the wooded ridge. This was the buck I was after. Everything was perfect: The wind was right, there was still more than enough light, and he was coming my way. The problem was that he was approaching from the wrong direction and would pass behind me if he continued on his path. No problem. I slowly swung around the tree and got into position for the shot. I was able to change trees quietly, move to the other side of the tree, and eventually get an easy shot because I was using an Ambush Sling.

I discovered the Ambush Sling about eighteen years ago, and this product dramatically changed the way I hunt. Bowhunting for mature bucks is all about being able to adapt to their ever-changing movements. Even though my plan is to have a tree ready for every potential situation, this does not always work. Bucks are very aware of hunting pressure and are always adapting to our movements. The more adept and expedient you are at responding to changing deer movement, the better your chances will be at tagging that trophy. Used in conjunction with conven-

Chris hanging in his sling (note crooked tree trunk).

tional and climbing tree stands, the Ambush Sling is a tool that is amazingly well suited to the pursuit of the unpredictable whitetail.

An Ambush Sling looks like a seat belt gone wrong and is similar to the type of harness rock climbers wear. The idea is simple: You hang in the sling from the trunk of the tree to which you are securely fastened. You sit facing the tree, with your legs somewhat straddling the trunk. To shoot, you lean back in the sling away from the tree. This is exactly the opposite position from that in conventional platform stands or climbers, and it takes some getting used to. There is no platform to stand on and nothing to encumber movement around the tree or make noise. Your feet rest on tree steps placed around the tree or on any branches that may be at the same level. They are used for leverage while maneuvering and as footrests while sitting. Once properly adjusted, the sling can be very comfortable. It acts as its own safety belt and is almost impossible to fall out of once properly fastened to the tree.

Not only can you adjust quickly to changing sign during the season, but you can also prepare as many trees prior to the season as you consider necessary. This is because you need only one Ambush Sling to hunt from all of your trees. You don't have to limit yourself to a handful of spots; you can prepare trees for every potential situation. At the beginning of every season, I have over fifty trees ready for hunting, the majority of which are set up for the sling. Only fifteen to twenty of them may get hunted during the course of the season, but if one of the setup spots heats up, I'm ready. Having so many trees ready to hunt is a huge advantage. On one twenty-acre piece of property that I've been hunting for years, I have eleven trees ready to go, including a couple in out-of-the-way locations that to this day have never been hunted, but they are in potential hot spots that I keep track of during the prerut and rut. Having so many trees ready for the season also allows you to rotate stands, which increases your element of surprise and reduces the scent contamination of the area. Truly pressured mature bucks do not tolerate hunter pressure. Rotating keeps your spots fresh and productive.

Another big advantage of the sling is that it makes it possible to shoot a full 360 degrees around your tree. Mature bucks often come to stands from unexpected directions, and this enables you to get a shot regardless of where it comes from. In hard-hunted areas, you'll rarely get a second chance at a mature buck. You have to make your shot opportunities count, and the Ambush Sling can put you in any position to do so.

The benefits of using a sling are numerous. With a sling, the number of trees from which you can hunt is greatly increased. It's no longer a question of finding an appropriate tree, but of finding the right spot and making a tree work. With conventional or climbing tree stands, you have limits as to the diameter of the trees, and they must be relatively straight. With climbers, you must choose trees devoid of branches on your way up. With a sling, there are no limits to diameter, branches, or straightness, although trees leaning more than 20 degrees will not give you the full 360-degree shooting arc.

The sling also gives you the ability to adjust to circumstances. If you find a hot scrape, it is no problem to quietly set up and hunt in a matter of minutes. This allows you to take advantage of fresh sign. Since the sling weighs only about one pound and rolls up into a four-inch round ball, it can be carried in any pack. This makes it easier to scout and set up at the spur of the moment. Try scouting a couple times with a tree stand hanging on your back while walking through brush, and you'll know what I mean.

Whenever I go on a trip to hunt unfamiliar areas, I take along several freelance fanny packs, each of which contains tree steps, reflective markers, screw-in bow holders, rope, and a hand saw. I usually take four of these packs for a one-week hunt. The first day, I scout and set up four trees, leaving the steps in each tree after it is set up. These trees are now ready to hunt without my having to carry or move any stands around. If I don't like one of these locations after hunting it, I simply take the steps out as I leave and keep that set with me in case I find another spot to hunt. Being able to move just twenty yards closer to a given spot can sometimes make all the difference in the world. Still another big advantage of the sling is that you can be sure your stand will be there when you arrive because it is in your pack. Stolen tree stands are unfortunately a sad fact of life for anyone who hunts state land, or even private property. You can also be sure no one will hunt your stands while you are elsewhere.

Yet another big plus is that you can keep the trunk of the tree that you are sitting in between you and the deer. As a deer approaches, you just slowly ease your way around the trunk, out of sight of the deer. This keeps your silhouette from sticking out from the tree, which is unavoidable with

Other than the extension saw, everything needed to set up a new tree for the Ambush Sling fits into what I call my freelance pack.

tree stands. Height is another big advantage. With a sling, the only height constraint is your ability to get up the tree. Attaching the sling is rather simple, and it makes much less noise than pulling up and hanging a tree stand or using a climber. While hunting mobile, the situation often arises where the best place to set up is close to a bedding area. The noise made setting up a stand can make all the difference in the outcome of a hunt.

As good as the sling is, it has a few drawbacks. For out-of-shape and larger hunters, the sling can be extremely uncomfortable. Of all the hunters I know who have tried a sling, many of them still use climbers or conventional tree stands in their main hunting locations for comfort reasons. About half of them use the sling for mobile hunting situations or for hunting with friends in unfamiliar areas. Most hunters rarely set stands more than twenty feet high, so with a sling in your pack, if a friend puts you in one of his "best" spots, you can set up above his tree stand in your sling with just a few tree steps. I've done this successfully on several occasions.

On a hunt in December 1988, a friend asked me if I would sit above one of his longtime tree stands. He told me there was a big doe in the area that would always spot him in his stand, stomp, snort for several minutes, spook every deer around, and then run off. Still the owner of an unfilled doe tag, I took him up on the offer. Hanging in my sling fifteen feet above his stand, I patiently waited for the encounter. Just as he described it, she came in and looked right up at his tree stand. I had moved around to the opposite side of the tree and was well above his stand, so she had no idea I was there. Being satisfied that nobody was in the stand, she continued on. Once past the tree, she offered me an easy fifteen-yard quartering-away shot, which I took advantage of. Another friend of mine did the same thing with a huge Illinois buck.

If you're satisfied with only a few stand locations, or have only one or two places to hunt, a conventional stand or climber can be a better option. A sling is much better suited to hunting travel routes and natural feeding areas than hunting over feeders or bait piles. With a sling, you have to adjust your legs and body occasionally, so setting up where deer are going to be standing around for long periods, such as around bait piles or feeders, could lead to your being spotted. The sling works better the higher up you are in your tree. I suggest sitting a minimum of twenty feet off the ground. If you don't like to hunt high up in trees, a conventional or climbing tree stand is a better option. The lower in the tree you sit, the closer you are to the deer's peripheral vision, and the more it matters that you remain perfectly still. This is especially true in heavily hunted areas, where deer tend to look for hunters in trees.

Preparing a tree for sling use is simple. When you locate a place where you would like to hunt, choose the best tree that is fifteen to twenty yards from your anticipated shot. Usually a midsize tree is best, but any size tree will work. I have hunted in trees ranging from six inches to three feet in diameter at my hunting height. I like to use at least twelve steps to get up to the appropriate height of twenty to thirty-five feet, depending on the foliage cover available at the time. When I reach my desired hunting height, I use anywhere from three to six steps (depending on the diameter of the tree), spaced evenly around the trunk of the tree to stand on. Having pulled on the Ambush Sling harness before starting up the tree, I then attach the sling lead strap to the tree at eye level or slightly above. Although I have modified the way I attach the sling to the tree for quicker adjustments, follow the directions for attachment that come with it. They work just fine. The length of sling lead between you and the tree is a matter of personal comfort and differs for each individual. Screw in bow holders for your bow, quiver, and pack to complete the setup. With a little practice, this entire process can be completed in a few minutes, and if your trees are prepared before the season opens, there is nothing to it.

The type of stand you use is ultimately based on your own hunting situation, goals, and personal preference. The Ambush Sling has completely changed the way I hunt, and I don't know how I could ever again hunt without it. I believe that using a conventional tree stand would cut my shot opportunities nearly in half. While the sling will not replace climbers or conventional tree stands, it's a tool that should also be in your arsenal for certain situations where you need increased mobility. If used properly, it can increase your chances of success dramatically.

CHAPTER 5

Scent Control

If I could choose to overcome only one of the whitetails' senses, it would definitely be their sense of smell. While their hearing and eyesight are extremely acute, a deer's nose is what gives most hunters fits. I am quite certain that if a poll were taken among serious bowhunters, the one thing they would like to have total control over would be their human odor. Under average weather conditions, a downwind whitetail deer can smell human odor from a quarter mile away.

When you hunt pressured areas, you simply have to be more meticulous about every aspect of your hunting, and that includes scent control. In my home state of Michigan, most mature deer will not tolerate any human odor whatsoever. At the first hint of human scent during deer season, they are gone. During my few hunts in states with far less hunting pressure, there was a big difference in how much human scent a deer would tolerate before it spooked. Deer that do not experience at least moderate hunting pressure simply are not as conditioned to human scent as a serious sign of danger. This means that a lapse in scent control might not have the same consequences as in areas that receive heavy hunting pressure. When I hunt on several pieces of property in Iowa that experience very little hunting, comparatively speaking the deer seem much less concerned with human scent. When hunting there I find myself becoming more lax with scent control, whereas normally I'm fanatical about it.

During my nearly forty years of bowhunting, I've gone through many learning processes: Learning to pay attention to my odor, to hunt in accordance with the wind, how to use commercial scents appropriately, and how to control odor in general have gone hand in hand with pursuing mature bucks. The older the buck, the more in tune he is to his surroundings, particularly odors in his core area. The presence of an unusual odor or human odor can cause him to become uncomfortable and adjust his behavior, making the probability of a shot opportunity much less likely. Thus it's important to keep all human scent out of a buck's core area, and if you use any other type of scent, do so appropriately and in moderation. When you hunt pressured mature deer, there is no room for error. Not paying enough attention to scent can be your biggest hindrance to regular success on mature pressured bucks.

CONTROLLING YOUR ODOR

With all the information about scent control out there these days, you would think that everyone would already be practicing it diligently. This is just not the case. I regularly see hunters in restaurants, gas stations, or cars wearing hunting clothes. All of these places are full of strong odors, which your clothing will pick up. Thus you should not wear your hunting clothes or footwear at any time or anywhere other than in the woods.

There are many items on the market that claim to help reduce or inhibit human body odor while hunting. Many of them work, but some, in my opinion, do not. Always shower before hunting or scouting, and use unscented soap and shampoo. Also use unscented deodorant. You may even want to shave your armpits. Hair holds moisture from sweat, allowing bacteria to grow and multiply rapidly, producing more odor. Brushing your teeth and tongue with baking soda will help reduce breath odor.

It is vital to wash all your hunting clothes frequently with an unscented detergent and to keep them in airtight containers until they are to be worn. The warmer the weather, the more frequently your clothing should be washed, due to increased perspiration. During extremely cold weather, wash your underlayers more often than your exterior layers. It's also a good idea to keep your external layers and underlayers in their own separate containers. This keeps the scent from your inner layers from contaminating your outer layers. Backpacks and fannypacks worn during warm weather will pick up body odor through your clothing, and should be washed regularly in unscented detergent as well.

Overheating will definitely make it more likely that the deer will catch your scent. When you start to sweat, you start to stink. Always layer your clothing so that you can adjust to the temperature and situation. Many hunters with whom I have hunted in the past wore all their gear while walking to their stands, even if they had to walk a half mile to get there. By the time they were on stand, they would be sweating profusely and unzipping all their clothes in an attempt to cool down. But by then it was too late; their undergarments were already wet with sweat. To keep this from happening, dress light while walking to your stand, and carry the rest of your clothing in a backpack. If you begin to overheat, remove a

Keep all clothing in airtight containers at all times, including your backpack.

layer and stow it in your pack. Once you get on stand and your body cools down, put on the rest of your clothes. Do not put them on at the base of your tree; this will leave unwanted odor on the ground. Human odor coming from twenty to thirty-five feet off the ground is much more difficult for deer to detect than odor left on the ground. If you are uncomfortable dressing on stand, you can put on your hunting clothes a couple hundred yards from your tree, and then stalk to your stand very slowly and quietly to avoid overheating.

It is extremely important not to touch any brush, trees, or weeds with your body or clothing while entering or exiting your stands. Any contact with foliage will leave some amount of human odor, and mature deer will likely detect it. While walking through tall weeds or traversing a thick swamp, you will not be able to avoid touching things. Try to be as scent-free as possible when you know you will have to pass through these types of terrain.

Activated Carbon Clothing

In 1996, I started using an article of clothing that has changed the way I hunt—an activated carbon Scent-Lok suit. There used to be areas I simply would not hunt, no matter what the wind direction. Some of those areas were sides of ridges, saddles, valleys, corners of fields when the leaves were still on the trees, and small openings in wooded areas. These were some of the locations where inconsistent swirling wind currents would occasionally tip mature deer off to my location, causing them to alter their movements. Once I started wearing a Scent-Lok odor-adsorbing suit (there's a difference between "adsorb" and "absorb"), it totally altered my thought process concerning the wind direction necessary to hunt those types of locations. After using odor-adsorbing carbon hunting suits for a few years, my confidence in them has become so strong that I will not hunt without one. Activated carbon suits give the hunter a huge advantage when pursuing game animals that rely on their sense of smell for survival.

Does an activated carbon suit help you get closer to mature whitetails on a regular basis? The answer to that question is absolutely, positively, yes! If properly cared for and worn in conjunction with odorless rubber boots, carbon-lined head cover, and a scent-free backpack, an activated Scent-Lok suit will absolutely amaze you. If it is not properly cared for, however, it is no more valuable than any other regular camouflage suit. Taking extremely good care of your Scent-Lok suits is the key to their continued reliable performance. Activated carbon technology and its effectiveness hinge on your dedication and desire to be scent-free. A properly cared-for suit will last for years.

When it comes to new hunting products and technology, I am definitely a skeptic. Before I buy anything new that is expensive, I gather all the available information about the product. And after a purchase, I try to test it thoroughly in all conditions. Even after using a Scent-Lok suit for several weeks without having been winded, I still was not completely convinced, so I attempted a little test. I decided to hunt a small piece of property near my home in central Michigan where the chances of killing a mature buck were very slim. On this particular property, there are two parallel runways about forty yards apart coming out of a small cedar swamp and leading to an alfalfa field. The deer traveled from west to east along these runways in the evening on their way to the alfalfa field. I had a tree cleared out along the northernmost runway. On my previous hunts at this location, there had always been does that used the runway to the south.

For the first part of the test, I wore my activated Scent-Lok suit. It was an evening hunt, and the wind was straight out of the north. Just as anticipated, a big doe stepped out of the swamp, walked past on the runway forty yards to the south, and did not spook in the least. The next night, I wore a camouflage cotton chamois suit. The wind was still out of the north, and everything happened just like the night before—well, almost everything. The difference was that when the same mature doe was directly downwind of me, she stopped, stared in my direction, and began to snort. She spent the next five minutes letting every deer in the county know where I was hunting. From that minute on, I was absolutely convinced that odor-adsorbing hunting suits are extremely effective. Since wearing my Scent-Lok suit, I see many more deer than I used to, and I often have deer downwind of me without spooking. In fact, I estimate that nearly half the deer I see while hunting are at some point downwind of me, and I have not been winded in years! I've had deer stop and sense something was not quite right, but within seconds they always continued on their way, evidently convinced that there was not any immediate danger.

So why are these suits so effective? Like most people, when they first entered the marketplace in 1992 I did not believe that an article of clothing could adsorb most of my human odor while on stand. After several years of hearing successful hunting stories I decided to research the carbon clothing technology prior to purchasing an expensive green liner. What I found was extremely enlightening.

Activated carbon is standard in many products that we use in our daily lives, including air filtration and exhaust systems. The military has also used activated carbon in protective clothing designed to prevent biological and chemical agents from reaching the skin of soldiers. Odor-adsorbing hunting suits are designed to keep scent molecules from being expelled through the suit and into the air, so that a hunter does not get winded.

Adsorption works to adhere liquid or gascous molecules to a surface in a thin layer, unlike absorption, which sucks up what is absorbed. Activated carbon is the most effective odor-adsorbing substance known to man. Our bodies are constantly producing scent molecules in a gaseous, solid, and liquid state. All Scent-Lok branded products have odor-adsorbing linings designed so that human odors, gases, and moisture pass through the fabrics, make contact with a layer of activated carbon, and are then expelled as filtered air. As these molecules pass through the layer of activated carbon they are attracted to the surface and interior pores of the carbon until they reach an area where they cannot go any further. The scientific name for this is the Van derwaal's bond. Will an odor-adsorbing hunting suit totally eliminate 100 percent of your odor? Not quite. But it will make you so odor-free that getting winded will virtually become a thing of the past.

From time to time, activated carbon clothing needs to be reactivated to remove the scent molecules it has adsorbed. Reactivation is done by placing the suit in a clothes dryer for twenty minutes on medium to high heat, or following the label instructions of whatever suit you purchase. The heat from the clothes dryer creates what is scientifically known as the Brownian molecular motion, which causes the trapped scent molecules to move rapidly. This rapid movement breaks the molecules free from the surface and interior pores of the carbon, eventually allowing them to exit the suit and the dryer.

If there is a strong odor left in the dryer from previously used perfumed softener sheets, dry a couple wet towels before reactivating your carbon suit. Most odor-adsorbing carbon hunting suits on the market have enough activated carbon to adsorb human odor molecules from multiple hunts before they need to be reactivated. Under normal weather conditions, I usually reactivate my Scent-Lok clothing after every six hunts. Any new Scent-Lok suit should be reactivated before using it. When an odor-adsorbing hunting suit sits on a shelf in a store, it adsorbs odors that need to be dispelled prior to use.

Once a suit has been reactivated, place it directly in a plastic bag, activated carbon storage sack, or airtight plastic tub. The suit should remain in one of these containers until it is to be used in the field. Return it to the container as soon as you are out of the woods, and before you climb back into your vehicle. Do not wear your suit while driving, getting gas, at home, in a restaurant, or anyplace where it can pick up foreign odors. Do not place scent wafers, pine boughs, or any other item with an odor in the container with your odor-adsorbing hunting suit; this will load up the carbon prematurely. Any layers that you will wear over your odor-adsorbing hunting suit should be washed with an unscented detergent and then stored in an airtight container in the same manner.

It's a good idea to have more than one head cover and to alternate them every one or two hunts. Your head expels a lot of scent molecules through hair follicles, mouth, and nose, so the head cover should be reactivated much more frequently than the rest of the odor-adsorbing clothing.

A Scent-Lok odor-adsorbing suit should be washed in an unscented detergent two or three times per season if used in a warm climate. When a Scent-Lok suit treated for moisture control is washed according to the garment's care label instructions, the majority of body oils that have adhered to the clothing (in the armpit, neck, forehead, and crotch areas) will be extracted from the suit. With untreated fabrics, most body oils will remain, which means that they will eventually saturate the clothing and go through onto the carbon particles, rendering those areas permanently nonadsorptive. Oil will not easily wash out of activated carbon particles. Considering that a hunting suit is worn in conditions where you are very likely to sweat, just think how much body oil could be entering your suit and saturating the carbon.

Moisture control treatment also gives the cloth excellent wicking ability, which adds to the overall comfort of the garment. By wicking moisture to a much larger surface area of cloth, moisture-control garments allow perspiration to evaporate more rapidly, adding to the overall comfort of the suit, especially during warm weather. At the same time, water-soluble body odors are spread over a larger area, thus allowing the odor molecules to make contact with more of the activated carbon particles in the odor-adsorbing linings. This helps to keep the suit from becoming saturated with body oils in heavy perspiration areas.

Rain Gear

Waterproof breathable odor-adsorbing carbon suits are also available, but I don't recommend these. Most waterproof breathable garments in the hunting industry have a Teflon or polyurethane membrane bonded or attached to the inside of a permeable exterior layer of cloth. The seams are then made waterproof by attaching tape or another piece of the same material over them. The idea of a breathable suit may bring to mind materials that allow enough airflow for perspiration to evaporate and for comfort during warm weather; unfortunately, waterproof breathable suits allow such a minute amount of air to pass through them that the word breathable is relatively meaningless.

A waterproof odor-adsorbing hunting suit, in which the activated carbon is permanently bonded to the suit or within the membrane, will in fact cause discomfort while hunting during warm weather and has some potential problems. To reactivate the carbon, the suit needs to be placed in the dryer periodically, but over time, the heat from the dryer can possibly delaminate the waterproof seams or the membrane from the cloth, causing the suit to lose its waterproof qualities. Therefore, with most waterproof carbon suits, you are in a no-win situation: If you do not reactivate the suit regularly, the carbon will load up and no longer be effective. But if you use the dryer to reactivate the carbon, the waterproofing could eventually be ruined.

My recommendation is to carry a quiet packable rain suit to wear over a permeable odor-adsorbing carbon hunting suit. This way you have an extremely breathable camouflage suit for everyday hunting and a rain suit to keep you dry if it should rain. You can simply let the packable waterproof suit air-dry when wet without fear of delaminating the waterproof membrane, and your carbon suit can be reactivated as needed. Quiet waterproof suits, uninsulated or insulated, are wonderful for hunting in the rain or for blocking the wind in cold weather.

Boots and Gloves

Clean rubber boots are an absolute must when hunting pressured deer. Boots that breathe leave odor; it's that simple. Rubber does not breathe, so odors remain inside the boots, and no human odor is left behind as you walk to your stand. When using carbon-lined suits, don't tuck your pant legs into the boots. Every time you take a step, a puff of air escapes out the top of the boot. With your pants over the boots, the carbon suit will adsorb the odor.

New rubber boots have an odor of their own that could alter a whitetail's routine or even spook him, as it's a foreign odor to game animals. So when you buy a new pair of rubber boots, let them air out in your garage for a year or pack them in mud for a week or so before you wear them hunting.

Before I began to wear rubber boots while hunting, I regularly had mature deer lock up immediately when they crossed my entry path. Their reactions were predictable. The does would stop, stomp their feet, snort, and then nervously leave. The bucks would just back up, turn around, and leave. Any other deer coming down the same trail would do the same thing at exactly the same spot. There is nothing worse than having a doe blow at you for ten minutes during prime time to totally ruin your hunt and your confidence. After I started wearing rubber boots, this no longer happened, as long as I was careful not to walk through grass or weeds that were taller than my boots. Rubber hip boots and chest waders also used to be part of my scent control arsenal if I had to walk through tall weeds to get to my stands. Now that I wear an activated carbon Scent-Lok suit, the rubber hip boots are no longer necessary for scent-suppressing purposes.

Boots are also made with permanent carbon liners, but the only way to reactivate the carbon is to place them in the dryer, and I don't think my wife would take kindly to having my boots thumping around in there. Due to the amount of odor expelled from your feet, they would need to be reactivated even more frequently than a head cover. I think it's a good idea to stick to rubber boots until the boot makers come up with something better.

I also recommend wearing activated carbon gloves while climbing to your stand so that no human scent remains on the bark or tree steps. In the past, I've had small bucks actually come to the base of my tree and smell my tree steps, and then spook.

USE OF SCENTS

In pressured areas, any change in a mature buck's environment can potentially change his daily routine, and that includes foreign odors. There are several mistakes that hunters make regularly. Sex scents used early in the season, apple, acorn, or pine scents used where none of these trees exist, or simply using too much scent are just a few examples of improper use of scents. Any one of these could be reason enough for a mature buck to alter his pattern and send him on his way. Another scent that has worked against me is skunk cover scent, which in reality is an alarm or danger scent. While it did not spook mature bucks out of the area like human odor would, it did alter their movements out of my shot range and immediately put them on alert, making them more aware of their surroundings. If you use scents, make sure you match them to the situation and the time of year. Sex scents should be used only during the prerut or rut. Do not use pine cover scent where there are no pines. And always use scents in moderation, as the directions imply. If you squirt half a bottle of scent on the ground every time you walk in the woods, after a few hunts this particular scent will become useless, and probably even detrimental to success. Mature bucks will recognize this overabundance of scent as being unnatural. If you have found a particular scent that works for you, then stick to it. Confidence in a particular product can actually have more to do with its success than the product itself. Although I am a firm believer that scents can and do work when used properly, I rarely use them. Scent use is very popular, and in heavily hunted areas, you can bet that the vast majority of hunters are using some type of scent. This can be devastating to its effectiveness. Frequent scent use causes mature bucks to associate strong scents with human activity and leads them to avoid certain areas altogether. Since opportunities at mature bucks in pressured areas happen so seldom, I always try to hunt counter to the normal hunting habits. Once a mature pressured buck winds any scent, he instantly becomes more aware of his surroundings, making it much more difficult for the hunter to go undetected. The only exception would be the proper use of a sex or intruder scent during the rut phases. I do not want a scent to suddenly change the mind-set, and potentially alter the movements, of a mature buck as he is freely following a set routine. Therefore, I prefer to concentrate my scent-related efforts on scent control.

Real Tarsal Glands
One form of scent that I do use regularly during all phases of the rut is real tarsal glands. Real tarsal glands and some commercial tarsal scents can work like magic in attracting the dominant buck in the area. When you or someone you know shoots a buck, cut off the tarsal glands, located on the inside of the hind legs, and save them for future hunts. You use them as follows: During the prerut, while on your way to your tree, stop about a hundred to two hundred yards from your tree, and fasten one of the tarsal glands to a string about six feet long with a safety pin. Drag the tarsal gland behind you the rest of the way to your tree, making sure to pass through at least one shooting lane. Then tie the tarsal gland to a branch about waist-high, in an easy-to-shoot location. Make sure you wear rubber boots and an activated carbon suit while dragging the tarsal gland. By doing this, you are leaving the scent of a foreign buck in the core territory of the local dominant buck. If the dominant buck crosses the scent trail and he is not with an estrous doe, he will more than likely follow the trail to investigate. By hanging the tarsal gland in the tree, the scent from the gland will be carried by the wind, and if the buck crosses this scent, he may come in to investigate the unfamiliar intruder.

The benefits of using real tarsal glands are obvious. You can be certain that you are using real scent that will have an effect on other deer. Because there is no bottle to squirt or capsule to open, you will not overdose the area with scent. It has also been my experience that does will not spook when they cross the scent trail of a real tarsal gland during the rut phases as they would prior to them. Tarsal glands are also free. Every year I shrink-wrap and freeze all the tarsal glands from bucks I shoot, and

After he followed a tarsal drag, this ten-point was taken in 1999 on a fifteen yard shot.

mark the year and time of season they were taken. I also save doe tarsal glands to use as cover scents early in the season and for scent drags along with the buck tarsal glands during the rut phases. Full-rut tarsal glands and doe tarsal glands can be found at any deer-processing operation during gun season. Try to get the ruttiest-smelling ones you can that are not rotten. Store the tarsal gland you are currently using in an airtight plastic bag in a refrigerator to keep it from spoiling when not in use. Once a tarsal gland starts smelling rancid, throw it away and start using a new one. I started using tarsal glands as a scent while hunting in the midseventies after witnessing bucks urinating down their hind legs over their tarsal glands to scent-mark scrapes. Most hunters in those days, and many these days as well, treated the tarsal glands as though they were poison, cutting them out because they believed the glands would taint the taste of the meat. The first time I took a good whiff of a stinky full-rut tarsal gland, I knew that it could be used to attract dominant bucks. I believe that tarsal glands are the best scent-related tactic you can use during the prerut phase for mature dominant bucks.

I have killed several big bucks using tarsal glands to lure them within range. A good example is a big ten-point taken in 1999. I had previously discovered a primary scrape area on a new hunting property while postseason scouting the previous winter. It was late October during the prerut before this spot was ready to hunt. The two previous times I checked for scrapes, there wasn't any activity, so I didn't hunt the property. This time, though, two fresh scrapes and several rubs filled me with anticipation for my first hunt in this excellent spot. Using a tarsal gland from another mature buck, I laid a scent trail along the edge of a weed field leading to my stand location near the fresh scrapes. By 5:45 P.M., I had not seen any deer, and my rattle bag was screaming at me to be called into action. About twenty seconds of rattling followed by a minute of sparring was all it took to arouse a buck from the bedding area. Once out of the weed field, the buck immediately caught the scent of an intruder he was not familiar with. As he approached, following the tarsal drag scent trail, he was so fully concentrated on it that he reminded me of a beagle on the hot track of a cottontail. That buck did not lift his nose off the ground for at least 150 yards. He was so intent on the trail that when he entered my shooting lane, I had to blat twice to get him to stop for a shot. In fact, he did not stop until he lifted his nose to smell the tarsal gland hanging from a branch. The instant his nose touched the tarsal gland, I released my arrow. It flew true and appeared to hit exactly where I had aimed, which I hoped meant that I had hit lungs or liver or both.

The buck darted about fifty yards before abruptly stopping behind some trees. Having a deer stop after a hit always makes you think negative thoughts. The only part of him visible to me was his hindquarters, and within a few minutes, he stepped totally out of sight. I've always been a believer in not going after an animal unless you are sure it is down, so I decided to remain in my tree for about another two hours. It was well after dark when I climbed down, and then quietly crept the fifteen yards to where the buck had been standing when I shot. Upon inspection, I could find neither arrow nor blood. Finally I found my arrow lying in the leaves about five yards away. After picking up the arrow, I turned around and left the scene. Close examination of the arrow made me feel confident that some vitals had been hit. One blade was very dull, probably from hitting a rib, which meant at least the liver was hit, if not a lung as well. After a long, semisleepless night, I recovered the big ten-point about twenty yards from where I last saw him. The tarsal gland scent trail had come through again.

Mature pressured deer may look at you or wind you for any of several reasons. It may be that you are sitting too low, not wearing odorless rubber boots, not wearing rubber or carbon gloves while climbing your tree, sitting over an unnatural bait pile, not having any back cover, not keeping your pack clean, or overhunting an area. Scent control is vital to pursuing mature bucks. Diligent scent control will greatly increase your odds of becoming consistently successful on mature bucks in both heavily pressured and nonpressured areas.

CHAPTER 6

Hunting Small Parcels

In hard-hunted areas, there is a lot of competition. You are limited to hunting where you can get permission, and this often means you are forced to hunt small parcels. By small parcel, I am referring to any piece of property under forty acres. This could even be a larger tract of land that has only a small patch of woods.

Nearly all the places I hunt are on parcels less than forty acres in size. I have permission to hunt parcels of twenty, ten, five, and even just a couple acres, and I've taken several good bucks on property less than five acres in size. In fact, I recently received permission to hunt a parcel of less than two acres. This property just happens to contain one of the best funnels that I have to hunt in. The property belongs to an acquaintance who sought me out to hunt there after his wife had had enough of the deer eating her shrubs and flowers.

While these tiny hunting spots are relatively rare to come by, often they are overlooked hot spots, or they border good private property and the deer cross through. Whatever the situation, any property where you can get permission to hunt is worth investigating, no matter how small. The old saying "Never judge a book by its cover" definitely holds true when looking for hunting property. You just might be surprised to find a mature buck living in or routinely passing through a tiny, previously unhunted spot that is surrounded by heavily hunted property. If a mature buck locates any decent cover in a small area without human pressure, he will more than likely turn it into his core bedding area or incorporate it into his travel route.

I started asking for permission to hunt on small parcels in the early eighties. Before that, I hunted strictly big-woods areas. The reason not to overlook hunting small parcels came suddenly. Chris was hunting near our home in central Michigan when he spotted a big buck cruising a fencerow the second day of archery season. This was unusual. First of all, the big ten-point was in an area of extreme gun hunting pressure in which any two-and-a-half-year-old buck was a rarity. And second, the buck was following a fencerow between a cow pasture and a tall weed field that led to a small swale behind a row of houses. The distance between the swale and the rest of the woods in the section was at least two hundred yards. After Chris told me about the buck, we went to investigate. Without mentioning the buck to any of the property owners, we asked at all the houses in the row for permission. We received permission to hunt ten acres. As luck had it, those ten acres were the buck's core bedding area. This buck had grown to maturity because he took up residence in a tiny area that had been overlooked. I hunted for the 140-class ten-point for two seasons before the landowner spotted the buck in his yard and decided he wanted to hunt the property himself. I never heard of that buck being taken; however, from that point on, I started to look for out-of-the-way small parcels.

If you are serious about hunting mature bucks anywhere, you have to prepare. If you are limited to hunting mature bucks on small parcels, you have to be absolutely meticulous with your preparation. On a large property, if a buck changes his pattern, you may be able to adjust and still eventually connect. On a small property, if you make a mistake, the buck you are after may change his routine, even slightly, and may leave or stop using the property, thus becoming out of reach. While hunting small parcels, you are also hunting a buck on his own terms. Usually you will have access only to a tiny portion of a buck's core area, if at all. You don't have the luxury of following all the best sign to the best spot. A buck's daily travel pattern might only cross through a tiny corner of the property. This means that you have to zero in on how and why a buck uses the property and try to be there when he is, without contaminating the property in the process. With this in mind, it's important to develop a plan for each individual small property and to make sure your setup is perfect.

Because it is even more critical not to contaminate a small piece of property than a large one, your scouting and stand setting must be completed in the early spring. This should be done between January and April, or in northern regions, as soon as the snow is off the ground. Traditional scouting just prior to the start of the season will alert any mature buck to your presence and could be reason enough to cause him to leave the property, or at least become nocturnal. It's always best to catch a mature buck completely by surprise in pressured areas; otherwise, your odds of taking him are slim at best.

When you scout small parcels in the early spring, take your time. Cover every inch of the land, looking for mature buck sign from the previous fall. If you always ask yourself why deer use a particular area the way they do and look for subtle nuances in their sign, you will be able to figure out how to hunt the property. Try to answer questions such as the following: Is there a bedding area on the property, or do the deer just pass through? Are deer using the spot in the morning or evening? Where are the nearest crops? What is the hunting pressure like on the property next door, and what effect will it have on the deer on this property? Do neighboring hunters hunt only on weekends or evenings? Does the sign indicate whether it would be better to hunt the area early or wait until the prerut starts later in the season? To consistently achieve success, you must have a plan, and by asking yourself these questions for every aspect of sign you find, you can begin to develop a plan for each small parcel.

Because the size of the property is limited, you should prepare trees for every possible situation. You may only hunt from a couple of these trees, but the others will be ready if any new sign shows up. You might notice a buck taking an unusual route. If you have a tree ready, this is a big advantage. Preparing the tree during season risks contaminating the area with your scent. On one thirty-acre piece of property, I have twelve trees ready to go at any time. This allows me to react quickly to changing deer movement. Prepare the best trees first—those in funnels between bedding areas and between bedding and feeding areas, in primary scrape areas, next to food mast trees, along rub lines, and in concentrated rub areas. Then work on trees in secondary spots, such as along runways or near water holes (if there are minimal water sources in the area). In most cases, you should not hunt along field edges unless a buck consistently passes by a specific tree. Your entries and exits when hunting field edges can rapidly alter a mature buck's movements into that field. There is too much chance of spooking deer while walking to or from your stand. Exceptions to this are when hunting along standing corn or tall weeds, both of which can provide cover as you approach or leave your stand.

If possible, it's a good idea to clear out a lookout stand. A lookout stand is a tree that you do not necessarily plan to hunt from, but from which you are able to observe deer movement at a distance. You should be able to approach and leave your lookout stand without spooking any deer. It's a good idea to sit in your lookout stand in the days just prior to the beginning of season. You may be able to locate the movement pattern of a mature buck still in his summer routine. The first few days of season will then be a golden opportunity to take this buck. The same procedure works well on larger properties as well. On small parcels, it is critical to keep human disturbance to an absolute minimum. Tactical planning is an important component to hunting small parcels correctly.

Hunting small areas with any hope of consistent success requires special tactics, which include a great amount of discipline and patience. Hunters make a common mistake when they find good buck sign or see a good buck on a small parcel, rush out and hunt the spot early (which can be fine), and then continue to hunt the spot regularly. This is a big and very costly mistake. Early in the season and throughout mid-October, a buck is more likely to be nocturnal than later in the season during the prerut and rut. By overhunting your best spots before this time, you are alerting mature deer, and that buck in particular, of your presence. That buck will more than likely pick up on the other mature deer's behavior and alter his movements accordingly. I believe that mature bucks become more nocturnal when the trees begin to lose their foliage. After several months of excellent cover, suddenly the woods become bare. At this time, bucks choose to move under the cover of darkness, whether there is hunting pressure or not. By hunting during this time, you can very well be informing a mature buck of your presence. This can be more than enough reason for him to avoid the area, thus reducing your chances for success. The more you hunt an area, the more sign you leave behind. The more deer that become aware of your presence and change their routine, the more likely it is that the buck you are after will change his routine as well. This means that it's just as important not to spook does as it is not to spook bucks.

If you have a small parcel where you know there is a mature buck, you could go about hunting as follows: If you have located the buck's movements early in the season from your lookout stand, you could hunt during the first day or two and try to intercept him while he is still in his summer routine. Then you should back off, be patient, and wait for the prerut. While you are waiting for the prerut to start, stay out of the area completely. The best thing you can do is hunt other places. If you do not have any other places to hunt, stick to secondary stands that are far enough away from your best stands that hunting them will not negatively affect your best locations. When the prerut arrives, wait for the perfect morning or evening to hunt, depending on which is better at your particular location. Now you can put on a little pressure and hunt a spot a few days in a row if the sign indicates activity. Remember, though, that each time you hunt a spot, your chances of success decrease. To avoid the downtime, I have numerous properties where I hunt. This allows me to rotate areas so that I do not overhunt any single spot. One of the biggest mistakes bowhunters make is simply overhunting an area. Too much pressure too soon allows a lot of mature bucks to survive the season.

Part of strategically hunting small parcels is knowing precisely when to hunt the area. If you have scouted thoroughly and determined why the deer use the property, you can plan exactly when to hunt. This can change considerably from property to property. Some places the best time is during the first week, others during the prerut, and still others not until late in the season. In one area I hunt, there are rarely any deer until after gun season. The deer, and more specifically, mature bucks, do not move into the area until they have been pressured out of their normal area by heavy gun-hunting pressure. The best time to hunt the property is early December. Every property is different and has unique circumstances. When you find sign, always ask yourself why the deer would act this way and then search for the answer. Only when you understand why the deer are using the property as they do, and discover a way to intercept this movement, will you be in a position to regularly take mature bucks on small parcels.

Nearly all of my hunting takes place on small parcels. A classic example of such a hunt was one that took place in late October during the prerut in 1995. I had received permission to hunt ten acres. These ten acres were situated between a large, half-moon-shaped bedding area around the back side of a small lake and an adjoining field that was overgrown and full of tall weeds and scattered brush. The property was also long, narrow, and bordered on one side by a busy road. While scouting the property the previous winter, I had discovered a scrape and rub line that was at least a 150 yards long and consisted of at least a dozen scrapes and twice as many rubs. The scrape and rub line was in thick cover, less than 100 yards from the road. Although I do not like to hunt field edges, in this case the best location to hunt this scrape and rub line was along the edge of the weed field. In mid-September, as I made my last-minute final stand touch-up, I noticed that the scrape and rub line was already active. This was a clear indication that the sign was being made by a mature buck.

The late-October afternoon was the first time I had hunted that location that season. I considered the scrape and rub line one of my most likely locations to kill a mature buck, so I waited until the prerut to hunt there. Hanging comfortably in my Ambush Sling, I watched several does and fawns pass by on their way to the tall weed field. Their final destination was a bean field at the opposite end of the weeds. When the does were out of sight, a fat little four-point burst onto the scene. He had his nose to the ground and was scent-trailing the does. He seemed to be in a big hurry, and just as fast as he arrived, he disappeared into the weeds. As the sun began to set, my anticipation grew. Several deer had passed through, completely unaware of my presence, which could almost be considered a prerequisite for a mature buck to move through.

Just after the sun dropped behind the horizon, I noticed a rack moving among the trees. The buck was approaching on the exact same route the four-point had taken, which meant he would pass within ten yards of my tree. He was closing in on me at a rapid pace and paying no attention to the scrapes. His interest was obviously focused on the does that had passed by earlier. As he stepped into my shooting lane, he was only ten yards away. I bleated to stop his quick pace. Being already at full draw, I released the instant he stopped. The hit was perfect, and the buck bolted. He covered about forty yards in a flash and crashed squarely into a young oak, where he expired. He had run into the tree with such force that he fractured his right G-2. Although the nice nine-point did not stop to freshen any of the scrapes, I was sure he was the buck that started the scrape line. I returned to that scrape line about a week later and found that it had become inactive. This confirmed my suspicions.

You are much more apt to find small parcels in suburban or semirural agricultural areas near cities than in big woods or timber areas. People are moving away from large cities and into the surrounding rural areas within an hour's drive from work. This leads to major property fragmentation. Many farms are being subdivided and sold off by the sons and daughters who inherit them. As the crop fields, fencerows, orchards, and pastures start to overgrow from nonuse, they create very good whitetail habitat. This is one of the main reasons why there are many more deer now in some rural agricultural and suburban areas than there were twenty to thirty years ago, when all the farms and orchards were being maintained and were well groomed.

Because semirural agricultural areas have an abundance of open ground, the deer have relatively few travel corridors. This is especially true once the crops in the area have been harvested, especially corn. Even the old, overgrown farms have a high percentage of open areas where mature bucks do not feel comfortable moving during daylight. In states with heavily populated semirural areas, a large percentage of the old fields that border roads now have homes built on them, thus shutting off even more land for the deer to move through. This forces the deer to use a much smaller portion of the available land. These semirural areas are becoming more populated at a very rapid rate. They also tend to be easier to hunt than heavily wooded or large areas of timber, because there is simply not as much cover for deer to bed in and travel through, making them easier to pinpoint. So when hunting in suburban or semirural areas, any property that has a defined travel route or funnel on it can be an outstanding place to hunt, no matter how small the parcel is.

CHAPTER 7

Other Hunters

In hard-hunted areas, you will have competition from other hunters. Considering the rate at which hunting land is disappearing, this has become a hunting fact of life, and it will only worsen as time goes on. In pressured areas, there will be other hunters on bordering properties, and usually on the same property that you hunt as well. You will encounter not only bowhunters, but gun hunters and bird hunters as well, and they all have the same rights as you. Most of these hunters will be polite and respectful, but others will be downright ruthless. Several times I've gone to hunt a particular tree that I recently cleared out, only to find someone else's stand hanging in it. The hunting pressure from others also influences the way deer move, and what other hunters do, good or bad, is completely out of your control. You have no choice but to deal with other hunters. How can you do so and still gain the advantage?

When you get permission to hunt new private property, always ask if others will be hunting the property. Ask the landowner how much the other hunters hunt, and when. Most hunters are predictable, and a landowner can be good source of information as to how and when they hunt. Quite often other hunters will hunt only on weekends. On such properties, I limit myself to hunting during the week, preferably Wednesday through Friday, when I will have the property all to myself and any deer spooked by weekend hunters will have had time to become less wary. It's also common for many hunters to hunt only evenings. If this is the case, hunt those areas primarily in the mornings and at midday. I prefer to stay as invisible to other hunters as possible. I respect them, let them do their thing, and try my best to hunt around them. If you are the only hunter with permission, offer to take responsibility for keeping unwanted people off the property, but get permission from the landowner first; you don't want to tell the landowner's visiting nephew to leave the property or make some other costly mistake. The landowner will usually appreciate the offer. This also relays an attitude of seriousness on your part that will be noticed by the landowner as well.

If you have done things as outlined earlier in this book, you will have gotten permission to hunt early in the year and started your scouting in late winter to early spring. This is the perfect time of year to be in the woods. You usually won't encounter other hunters, and you won't mess up their stands with the scent left by your presence. Besides looking for deer sign, also look for the previous year's hunter sign when you scout. It's just as important to pattern the other hunters as it is to pattern the deer. Deer will react to all hunting pressure on a piece of property, and it can only be to your advantage to know exactly where and how other hunters hunt the property. The majority of hunters will be average hunters who are out for a bit of recreation and are not all that serious. These hunters generally hunt the same couple stands all the time, are easy for deer to pattern, and are usually not a danger to mature bucks. They often have little bowhunting knowledge and, as far as you are concerned, should be seen as deer deflectors that deer simply move around.

One of the first things I look for is trails, paths, or two-tracks. Most of the time, hunters set up their stands very close to any trail on the property, and often trails will lead directly to stands. Cruise all trails, and note the locations of any stands on your scouting map while recording any other relevant information. Also look for signs of how the hunter hunted. Are his trees in good spots, are they prepared properly, and are his stands high enough? Has the hunter gone through the trouble of clearing out shooting lanes other than the trail he is set up on? It is surprising how many stands are in good spots, but the hunter would not be able to get a clear shot at an animal if his life depended on it. Another common mistake is the positioning of the stand on the wrong side of the tree, away from where the obvious shot would be. All these signs help indicate what sort of hunter is on the property and what kind of competition you are up against.

One thing I've noticed throughout the years is that most hunters do not often walk very far to their stands. Most bowhunters, no matter how big a parcel they hunt, sit in stands close to a road or two-track. In our computer-powered, fast-food, supersized world, people in general, including many hunters, seem to have become lazy. Most of the time, the farther back in the woods you go, the better your chances will be at finding mature bucks and less hunting pressure. On the flip side is the fact that most hunters will not hunt within a hundred yards of a main road or highway. In many instances, the first hundred yards along major highways is a seriously overlooked hot spot. Hunters will hunt on a lane or two-track in the woods but will stay away from major automobile traffic zones, assuming the traffic spooks the deer. This assumption is false and allows quite a few bucks to grow to maturity. Deer grow accustomed to the sounds of the traffic and, if there is adequate cover and little pressure, will bed very close to major highways. In the last ten years, I've taken several bucks within a hundred yards of a major highway or expressway. A buck I took in mid-October 2001 is a good example.

It was early October, and I was driving down one of Michigan's interstate highways en route to a 9:00 A.M. appointment. As always, my attention was focused partially on driving and partially on looking out the window for deer. After seeing several does during the first half hour of light, I noticed a large deer moving down a weedy fencerow bordering a large woodlot. Instinctively I honked my horn to get it to raise its head, and to my pleasant surprise, it was a very nice buck. I looked at the next mile marker and made a note to see about acquiring permission to bowhunt on my way back through. At about noon, I returned to the nearest exit, which was only about a half mile away from where I saw the buck, planning to drive around the section looking for a house that appeared to belong to the same property. I was honestly expecting to knock on someone's door and be refused hunting permission. But you never know unless you ask, so I was going to give it a try. As I turned the corner off the ramp, I had to take a second look before I could believe my eyes: There were state land signs all along the side of the road I wanted to hunt. In this particular area, there is very little state land, so this came as quite a surprise.

Parking in the guard-railed parking area on the opposite side of the section from where the buck was, I could not help but notice how muddy and in disarray the parking area was from so much hunting traffic. But being a believer that you never know what to expect until you check it out, I pulled on my scouting pack and took off through the woods. No ATVs are allowed in the area, and this became more obvious the farther I walked from the parking lot. Halfway through the section, the sign of human activity dwindled dramatically. I saw several tree stands within the first quarter mile of the parking lot, but there were none to be found across the section near the expressway.

With the nearly mile-long march back to where I had spotted the buck behind me, I started to walk along the fence where he had been moving earlier that morning. I had covered only about a hundred yards when the buck stood up in a small patch of tall weeds, looked at me, then quietly loped off into the woods. He carried a heavy, eight-point rack. The small patch of tall weeds was surrounded by a little strip of red brush and was right next to the fence not forty yards from the busy expressway. This reinforced my belief that a buck will bed nearly anywhere if there is enough cover and he is not being bothered. A quick inspection revealed a lot of hair in the bed, and that the weeds were matted down in a large area. This spot was definitely one of his regular bedding locations. And trust me, even though I was on state land, not many hunters walk along that fencerow. Since there were no trees within comfortable shooting range of the bed, I decided to scout the area and look for a rub line or scrape area, which is the type of sign I prefer to hunt. After a very short walk, I found "the spot." This was all unfolding way too easily. From my stand location, I could see seventeen rubs and ten scrapes. It was surprising to see a primary scrape area that active so early in the season.

The tree I selected was only eight inches in diameter at the twenty-eight-foot height from which I would hunt, but it was the only tree big enough to hunt from within shooting distance of the majority of sign. Knowing that this was a spot I would not be hunting more than twice, I wanted to hunt from a tree in the middle of the scrape area, even though there were bigger trees with more cover around the perimeter. On short-term hunts, you must be in the middle of the action, not on the edges. This location had every key sign one looks for. It had a rub line leading to it, it was obviously a primary scrape area, and it was also a staging area due to its location on the edge of a change in terrain. There was a small oak ridge loaded with acorns to the north, a bedding area to the south, the freeway 120 yards to the west, and a mile of relatively open mature hardwoods to the east.

My first opportunity to hunt for the eight-point was on the evening of October 16. The weather was not that great, there were gusty high winds, and it was raining. Bucks like to move during light rain, but not so much during high winds. However, in hunting there is only one guarantee: You can't kill anything if you're not there. So off I went. While walking the last hundred yards to my tree, I dragged a tarsal gland on the ground that I had saved from the previous year. I then strategically placed the tarsal gland fifteen yards from my tree in an easy shot location, which would require very little body movement to make a shot.

I settled into my sling at 3:30 P.M. The next couple hours were uneventful. At 6:30, I decided to do a rattling sequence, even though it could not be heard from very far away due to the heavy wind. Within five minutes, a nice little eight-point stalked into view about forty yards away. The wind blowing through the weeds and branches definitely made him nervous. He cautiously moved to within fifteen yards of me, looking for the bucks he thought he had heard fighting. When he got directly downwind of the tarsal gland, he froze briefly and then spooked. I guess he did not like the smell of the dominant full-rut tarsal gland. It's always interesting to see how does and bucks of different ages react to various tactics during the course of the season.

Darkness was starting to settle in as seven does and fawns walked into the dominant buck's zone. A button buck fawn's curiosity got the best of him, and he thoroughly investigated the tarsal gland hanging from the branch. He would take a sniff and then look at his mom as though he had just found something that she should come over and check out. He did this several times. Mom, however, did not seem to take even a slight interest. I thought it was unusual that none of the does paid any attention to the tarsal gland. Does generally take an interest in the scent of buck tarsal glands that early in the season and sometimes are even spooked by the smell.

The does were not there for more than three or four minutes before I heard a buck grunting over in the direction of the highway. As he approached, it was obvious he was the large eight-point I was pursuing. The does noticed him coming and started to scatter to the downwind side of my tree, and the buck went after the lead doe. I was glad to be wearing a Scent-Lok suit, because the buck was suddenly twenty yards straight downwind of me. I immediately drew my bow and shot right over his back. The arrow never touched him. Yep, a total miss! Though in a mild state of shock that I had missed a twenty-yard shot, I quickly nocked another arrow, just in case. After the shot, the buck took three jumps and moved only about ten yards before he stopped. Because of the wind and rain, I don't think he knew what had happened. The does were totally out of sight, but he just stood there checking out the surroundings for what had made the noise. Now that he was paying attention to his surroundings, he winded the tarsal gland and immediately started walking curiously toward it. When he was at a distance of fifteen yards, I took my second shot. This time I didn't miss. The shot was perfect, and the buck ran only fifty yards before making that unmistakable sound of a deer crashing to the ground while running at full throttle. The fine eight-point had an eighteen-inch inside spread.

The circumstances that led me to this buck were unusual but reinforced my belief that mature bucks have no qualms about living very close to major thoroughfares. This situation also reconfirmed my beliefs about how good hunting is during somewhat inclement weather. Most hunters don't like to hunt in a steady rain, so whenever the opportunity presents itself for me to hunt in adverse weather conditions, I do. A steady light rain or snowfall is a great time to be in the woods hunting. Mature bucks feel very comfortable moving during both of those conditions. Heavy rainstorms and high winds are about the only weather

This eight-point, taken on state land based on a highway sighting, returned to check out a tarsal gland even after my first shot missed him.

conditions in which I have rarely seen mature bucks, although I have hunted in both of them and still do occasionally.

Once you have thoroughly scouted your property for deer and hunter sign, a pattern should become visible. You'll likely notice that the other hunters set up in easily accessible locations that offer good deer sign, especially in open areas or along field edges. In many instances, they set up near sign mature bucks make only in the security of darkness. Many hunters even use quads to get within short walking distance of their stands; that is unacceptable when pursuing pressured mature bucks. Deer hear the quads and associate them with humans. Big bucks in pressured areas will not move before dark if they know there is human activity in the area, and the noise of a quad before daylight will usually push a mature buck back into cover prematurely. In such cases, look for the alternate routes deer take during daylight or evening hours to avoid these areas. The sign might not be as extensive and the runways not nearly as worn, but you want to find these trails in order to find the mature bucks. Follow this alternate trail or brush line and find out exactly where it leads. Clear out a spot on this alternate route and decide on the best time to hunt the spot.

When you set up your tree in an area frequented by other hunters, keep your location as inconspicuous as possible to prevent others from

Isolated sign such as this runway crossing a ditch can produce, but without other sign to back it up, it could prove very inconsistent.

finding and using your trees. Cut the saplings in your shooting lanes close to the ground, and try to set up the location in early spring so that new growth will make your lanes look more natural. The best time to hunt such a spot is usually during the prerut and rut. By then other hunters will have more than likely overhunted their stands, and the deer will have patterned their movements around them. If the bucks had an established nocturnal routine by this time (prerut), they should start moving again during daylight hours.

Another thing I regularly encounter is other hunters who set up on isolated sign. This may be a single well-used runway, a couple rubs, a single scrape, or a field edge with a runway passing by the tree. In such cases, the hunter found a piece of sign that looked good and placed his stand in that spot although the sign was isolated from other sign or there was a much better spot nearby. These hunters have usually failed to scout thoroughly enough to realize they are slightly out of position. Usually these stands are in an area where the hunters will see a lot of deer, even though most of them are not within shooting range. Seeing deer makes hunting enjoyable, but the chances of shooting a mature buck from such locations are slim. That hunter will probably leave his stand in that spot because he sees deer regularly. When I find stands in such positions, I simply look for alternate routes with mature buck sign. Before the main rut, I like to be set up along or in heavy cover where there is a concentration of sign. During this period, mature bucks like to move through areas with quick, easy escape routes that provide excellent cover. Once the rut starts, bucks will follow an estrous doe just about anywhere.

During October, when the trees begin to lose their foliage, bucks naturally become more nocturnal, with or without hunting pressure. They have spent the entire spring and summer in thick cover, and all of a sudden the cover disappears. Areas that were secure become open. Bucks react to this change by becoming more, or exclusively, nocturnal, and pressure from other hunters in the area just makes this happen much sooner. The only reason bucks change this pattern is out of sexual necessity. By the time prerut arrives, other hunters will usually have the mature does and bucks conditioned to their presence, and the deer will be using alternate routes. Use this to your advantage by letting the deer pattern any other hunters in the area and waiting until the prerut to hunt alternate routes. You may be surprised at the positive outcome.

Of course, when hunting property on which other hunters, whom you do not know, have permission, you are going to get frustrated occasionally. When you save a stand location for the prerut, only to find another hunter has set up so close that the spot is ruined from his overhunting, it is depressing. Unfortunately, there's nothing you can do about it. This is another reason multiple locations are necessary when hunting pressured property.

BAITING

The use of bait by other hunters is another situation you will encounter, both where it is legal and where it is not. Bait alters deer's natural movements dramatically, especially when it is used on a large scale. This is the case in Michigan, Wisconsin, Texas, as well as parts of Canada, and many other states, where hunting has almost become synonymous with baiting. Baiting requires little knowledge of deer or the woods, and it tends to make hunters complacent. It also is generally detrimental to consistently killing mature bucks in truly pressured areas. When others are baiting, it cannot be ignored and must be dealt with. For example, if the neighbors are baiting heavily, they could potentially pull a lot of deer from the property you are hunting onto their land, thus completely altering the natural movement pattern. This is especially true if the property you are hunting does not have a bedding area or natural food source on it. This has caused a lot of hunters to feel as though they have to bait on their property in order to counter the neighbor's baiting. The hard fact is that large bait piles attract mature does, and when the rut starts, the mature does attract the mature bucks. This is when the majority of mature bucks are killed near bait piles.

Most bait hunters set up within one hundred yards of a road or two-track so they don't have to carry the bait any farther than they have to. They know that deer will eventually come to the bait. They will set up in the same place year after year, leaving a nasty scar on the ground that is easily identified while scouting during the off season. Three-and-a-half-year-old and older bucks are not usually taken from bait piles in agricultural areas, where there are other abundant food sources. Most mature bucks that do visit a bait pile do it under the security of darkness. They have most likely experienced hunters sitting over bait since they were fawns and understand what the game is all about. Also, most bait hunters are guilty of overhunting their stands. They do this for several reasons, including the expense of bait and regular deer sightings. This allows mature does and bucks to pattern them rather easily. In fact, I have seen a mature doe completely circle a bait pile, and then stand about sixty yards out and stare intently at an empty tree stand for at least twenty minutes before she would approach the bait. I witnessed this in December one year while hunting for a big woods buck in a finger of cedars. The bait pile was on the neighboring property about a hundred yards across a clear-cut. After dark, mature bucks either use bait piles themselves or, during the rut phases, cruise from bait pile to bait pile looking for estrous does. If you are aware of this situation, you can hunt accordingly.

At this point, you have to make a decision: You can ignore the bait and hunt as though it were not there, or you can use the bait to your advantage by treating it as a normal food source and intercepting the deer before they get to it. There usually are defined runways leading to and from active bait piles. The ones with rubs along them are the ones to hunt first. If you're strictly pursuing mature bucks, hunting travel routes to bait should be productive, as nearly all deer will pass right by you without even noticing your presence. Because you will be on a travel route instead of at a destination point, you are less likely to be detected. Deer are much more alert when they near their destination point than when they are en route to it. The person who is doing the baiting will probably not be aware of your presence either.

When you find an area that is being baited, follow the runways back to a bedding area. Set up a stand as close to the bedding area as you can, or at a point somewhere in between the bedding area and the baiter, far enough away from both that you will not disturb either the bedded deer or the hunter. During the rut phases, mature bucks generally hang back out of bow range and allow other deer to approach the bait first. If you are a hundred yards or more away from the bait, the buck will come by you first. You also can be effective by hunting deer trails leading to and from bait at odd times. If the person doing the baiting is set in his routine, the deer will know this, and by hunting during midday, you may just get a chance at a large buck. Big bucks move during the midday in the rut phases.

SMALL-GAME AND BIRD HUNTERS

Small-game and bird hunters also can potentially alter the way you have to hunt. While these hunters have just as much right to hunt their target species as you do, their presence can alter the way or the locations you must hunt. Pheasant hunters have the most effect on the areas where I hunt. This is because mature bucks like to bed in overgrown tall weed fields, which is also where bird hunters hunt. These fields of tall weeds are safe havens for deer to bed in. Mature bucks will usually tolerate being temporarily pushed out of such a bedding area by a bird hunter once or twice. If a weed field is getting bird-hunted more frequently than that, a buck will normally find another place to bed. Squirrel hunters cause similar problems. They concentrate on the hardwoods, especially oaks and beech trees. The noise they make and the scent they leave behind can be enough to push a buck into nocturnal habits or into a different bedding area, and this is generally done in September prior to archery season opening. Preseason squirrel hunting will more than likely change the consistent summer pattern of any mature buck in the immediate area, making your opening day ambush unlikely.

Countering small-game hunting can be difficult or impossible if your hunting permission is limited to a small area. About the only thing you can do is hunt in other areas of the property when you know small-game hunting has taken place. Setting up near an alternate bedding area could allow you to catch a buck that has been pushed from one bedding area to another. When you know someone will be bird-hunting on a particular day, try to set up along an escape route or the deer's normal entry or exit route. Setting up on escape routes works especially well when the bird hunters are hunting a standing cornfield. They can actually push deer in your direction. And in such a situation, an otherwise nocturnal mature buck may be forced to move during daylight. One of the biggest bucks I've ever seen was pushed out of a tall weed field by pheasant hunters, but unfortunately the 170-class twelve-point departed in another direction from where I was sitting. I had never seen this buck before and never saw him again. Small-game hunting can definitely affect your deer hunting. Rather than getting mad, since you can't do anything about it, try to use it to your advantage as much as possible. Most of the time, the only option is to avoid hunting the property for a few days after small-game hunters and hope deer movement resumes as normal.

In many midwestern states where bowhunter numbers are extremely low, such as Iowa, Nebraska, and the Dakotas, the hunting actually improves after pheasant season opens. The mature bucks take up residency during the summer in the large fields, and when bird hunting season opens, they get continually pushed out of them. The bucks are then forced to find whatever cover they can, which is usually in river and creek bottoms, since most other land is used agriculturally. Once forced into these long, narrow areas of cover, they are extremely vulnerable and predictable, which makes them very easy to hunt and kill. This same scenario can also make hunting in heavily pressured states better if the property has little cover and many fields that get bird-hunted.

CORNFIELDS
In pressured areas, mature bucks will be much fewer than in nonpressured areas. Sometimes you have to look in unusual places to find them. Look for spots that have been overlooked by other hunters. In agricultural areas, standing corn is a key element in a deer's life that gets relatively little hunting pressure, especially during bow season. When the woods are full of hunters, head for the standing corn. Ground blinds or stalking in cornfields are techniques you need to have in your repertoire if you live in an agricultural area. Deer, and indeed mature bucks, head for the corn when hunting pressure begins in the woods. Dominant bucks will often take up residence in the corn and attempt to keep all other bucks out.

One area I hunted for several years with a great deal of success was a narrow draw that extended quite far out into a large field. One end of the draw tapered down to a point of tall weeds, while the other end bordered a subdivision and woodlot with old apple trees scattered throughout it. There was always a primary scrape area near the point of the draw and scattered scrapes throughout the woodlot. It was a mature buck hot spot. It was also the only area with trees and brush in a virtual sea of corn and beans, and therefore a meeting point where deer could make rubs and ground scrapes. The point of the draw was so far from any woods that no other hunters ever bothered to even look at it. The wooded area did get hunted, but the other hunters usually set up along the edge of the woods, which did not hinder my hunting whatsoever. In fact, it made the point I hunted much better. This spot unfortunately was further developed and is now covered by buildings.

I took this ten-point at the end of a draw in a primary scrape area. This land is now a subdivision.

Always look for ridges with oaks, brushy fencerows, small clumps of trees with underbrush, or even single fruit-bearing trees in standing corn-fields. A single acorn-producing oak in a standing cornfield can be a spot that can only be described with superlatives. Any opening or structure in a cornfield will attract deer, not necessarily as a bedding location as much

A pop-up blind set up in a cornfield, concealed using cornstalks, can produce big bucks. Make sure the farmer approves your use of the land.

as a pass-through location. These small spots are definitely worth investigating and are usually overlooked by other hunters.

Stalking the corn is another possibility and is one of my favorite tactics. The best time to stalk is midday, when most of the deer are bedded. There is no need to have an arrow nocked when stalking corn, as you will have ample time to back into the last row to get ready. Having an arrow nocked will actually slow down the stalking procedure. You begin a stalk by walking into the wind or crosswind perpendicular to the rows. When stalking in a crosswind, which is my preference, always start at the downwind side of the field. Moving very slowly, look into each approaching row both right and left. If you see no deer, step into that row and continue on in the same manner. Continue this process until you've completed a pass-through of the field, then move fifty yards down the field edge and stalk back to the other side. Continue until you've covered the entire field. Rubber boots and an activated Scent-Lok suit worn under a light beige suit that blends well with the corn are advised.

In hard-hunted areas, cornfields become sanctuaries for mature bucks and are the reason a lot of mature bucks remain alive for yet another season. If you see a deer while stalking, chances are it will be bedded. If the deer is one that you want to shoot, step back a couple rows, sneak into

Sights like this are common when stalking corn under the right conditions.

range, and step cautiously into the row the deer is in, ready to shoot. If the deer is one you don't want to shoot, move back a couple rows, sneak far enough away from the deer that you can cross the row without being detected, cross the row, and return to stalking. At this point, be extra careful. When you see one deer, there are usually others nearby. A doe could have a mature buck bedded very close by, especially during the rut.

As with all other tactics for mature pressured bucks, wait for the perfect situation and weather to stalk. I like to stalk on days that are windy and wet, or even during a hard rain, and preferably after a fair amount of hunting pressure has been put on neighboring woodlots. You must have noisy conditions for this method to work with any regularity. Stalking dry corn on calm days is nearly impossible, and your odds of getting a shot at a mature animal are just about zero. Take advantage of the situation and weather, stalk, and then leave the area alone. Never overdo it. Stalking corn can be a fun way to spend the day between morning and evening hunts. Although corn stalking is a simple and fairly well-known tactic, it is seldom practiced with archery equipment. When the woods are full of hunters, it can be a good idea to head for the corn.

When you hunt mature bucks, you have to be opportunistic. If you hunt property bordering a large cornfield, try to find out when the farmer is planning to cut or pick the corn. This can be a golden opportunity that you should mark on your calendar. If the cornfield is large enough, there is a good chance the local dominant buck will have taken up residence there. The combine will push the deer out. In this situation, it's best to hunt woods that border the corn directly so the deer can leave the field and remain in cover. Try to be in your stand before the farmer begins to cut, and remain there until he is finished or it gets dark. In small fields of twenty acres or less, usually the first couple passes of the combine are all it takes for deer to leave the field, but in areas with really heavy hunting pressure, I've seen deer wait until the farmer began to cut the last six rows before they bolted for cover. In any case, it pays to remain on stand as long as possible. A couple years ago, I set up for an evening hunt in a brushy funnel near a cornfield. I had just settled in when the farmer entered the field with his combine. That evening, I had five bucks casually walk out of the corn and directly under my tree.

GETTING AWAY FROM OTHER HUNTERS
One way to find undisturbed places with mature bucks is to get beyond where other hunters are willing or able to go. Three tools I sometimes use to get me to these places are my mountain bike, canoe, and chest waders. Aware of the fact that most hunters do not walk very far from their vehicles, I began to look for gaps in hunted areas, especially in areas where there are trails but motorized vehicles are not allowed, such as along Michigan's rails-to-trails system. These trails often allow access to small patches of state land that are either farther from a road than most people are willing to walk or landlocked by private property. I considered my options as to how to get into these places and eventually, with the timely

and coincidental purchase of a new mountain bike, came up with an idea. The mountain bike has since become an important part of my hunting equipment. For those interested in making the extra effort and finding new and relatively undisturbed hunting spots, a mountain bike provides excellent access on the trails that are abundant throughout many states. The modern mountain bike is quiet, versatile, and rugged enough that it allows you to go where motorized vehicles are not allowed or in some cases simply cannot travel. It is lightweight, and quick-release wheels allow it to fit easily into the backseat of a car or the bed of a truck.

My son Jon hunts heavily hunted state land and uses a mountain bike to get back in a mile or so farther than any ATVs are allowed, and he takes a good buck every year with little or no competition from other hunters. The hunting pressure on the easily accessible portion of the state land actually pushes some of the deer to the back of it.

State land is often full of trails that are sometimes easily traveled with a vehicle and sometimes not. Logging can turn a formerly good trail into a mud pit, essentially cutting off access to most hunters. But with a bike, the impassable trail is not a problem. Simply walk around the bad spots, and then continue riding.

A bike is also excellent for scouting. If you have a large piece of private property with trails to scout, the bike provides an expedient way of getting a good overview of the land. I discovered most of the places where I use my bike to hunt on evening rides during the summer. And using your bike to look for places to hunt sure makes staying in shape a lot more interesting. Another advantage is the noise factor. Riding a bike down a trail is nearly silent and will not disturb an area like an ATV or a truck would. I like to feel as if I'm sliding silently into a buck's realm, and he has no idea anything is going on.

Besides the bike and the will to get beyond the range of most hunters, there are only a few things needed to make hunting with the aid of a mountain bike an enjoyable and comfortable experience. One item of utmost importance is a headlight, available at any bike shop. I also carry a couple small flashlights so that if my headlight goes dim, I can hold a flashlight across the handlebars. A light that you wear on your head works just as well. Trust me, trying to ride your bike through the woods in the dark without a light is no fun.

A medium-size pack is another necessity for using a bike to hunt. The pack has to be large enough to accommodate the tools you need for the hunt—flashlights, rope, scent cover spray, drinking bottle—and just about all of your warm clothes. It is very important not to overheat and sweat on the way to your stand, so wear only one layer while riding, and take a

Mountain bikes can help you get farther away from other hunters, who will tend to stay along the perimeter of a property.

slow to moderate pace. There should be a nylon loop or handle on top of the pack for attaching your bow while you ride. I tie a two-foot-long piece of rope to my riser at one end, run the rope through the loop on my pack, and tie it to the other end of the riser. This way the bow is fastened securely to the back of the pack, and my hands remain free for riding. The extra rope allows me to shift my bow to one side of my body or the other if the trail gets narrow. Another possibility is to wear your stand with your pack and bow attached to it (this is easier with a Ambush Sling, which does not have the weight and bulk of a tree stand). This setup is a little awkward, so I recommend having all your stands in place before riding in. The first time I tried riding with a bow strapped across my back, I felt a little silly, but this changed when I found deer—many more than usual—far away from the masses, as calm as if they had never seen a hunter in their lives.

If you take your bike into the woods, you'll also need a way to lock it to a good-size tree. A cable lock is probably best; these are generally long enough to go around a tree, through the bike frame, and through both rims. The lock is necessary if you leave your bike some distance from, and out of sight of, your stand. Mountain bikes are not cheap, and this will give you the peace of mind that your bike will still be there when you want to make your return to civilization.

It's important to keep your bike in good working order so that you will not have any trouble in the field. Have your bike tuned before hunting season so that you can be sure it will stand up to the abuse. You also need to be in good condition. Hitting the trails and going after deer with a mountain bike requires physical fitness and the will to step beyond the normal limits that bowhunters set for themselves.

A canoe or boat is another excellent way to get to unpressured areas on both state and private land. Like a mountain bike, it can get you to remote locations that other hunters simply cannot access. Any river or lake usually offers a means of accessing property that may be otherwise inaccessible. It is also common to have bedding areas border the edges of rivers and lakes, with the only way to quietly access them being from the water.

It is important that you traverse the water very quietly, especially once you near your destination point. Foam-lined canoes are much quieter than heavy-gauge aluminum canoes, and most have exterior shells made of very thin aluminum and weigh less than fifty pounds, which means that they are easier for one person to load and handle. Such canoes are made for use with normal paddles, oars, or electric trolling motors. In some circumstances, oars or a trolling motor are better than a paddle. Square-stern canoes are my preference, because you can mount a trolling motor or small outboard to them if the need arises. Take a cable lock with you so that your canoe will be there when you return.

Always look for standing water. Most hunters will not cross water that is more than a few inches deep. This means that a river or larger stream, swamp, or even some ditches will keep hunters out of an area.

Crossing water can provide access to unpressured areas, such as the island where this buck was taken.

The deer will definitely be aware of the safety zone the water provides and will react to hunting pressure by moving across the water and remaining there until after dark. If you are prepared for this situation, you can use it to your advantage. A pair of camouflage neoprene waders or hip boots should be part of your hunting equipment. Carry your waders with you to the water, pull them on, cross the water, and then change back into your boots. Hide your waders, and proceed with the hunt. Hip boots or waders can also allow you to reach islands in marshes that are otherwise inaccessible. Two of my biggest bucks came from islands in cattail marshes on state land. Both of those spots could be reached only by wading through waist-deep water.

TIMING

You can also use other hunters' timing to your advantage. Most hunters follow a predictable pattern. If someone hunts in the morning, he arrives just before daylight or, worse, just after first light. He sits for a couple hours until 9:00 or 10:00 A.M., and then leaves. In the evening, he arrives a couple hours before dark, and then departs a few minutes before or after dark. He often spooks deer while approaching his stand in the morning and leaving it in the evening. This pattern does not go unnoticed by mature deer, and in areas of heavy hunting pressure, it can be used to your advantage.

Head for your stand when the other hunters are leaving, which means you will be entering the woods around 9:00 A.M. You will be surprised how many deer move between 10:00 A.M. and 2:00 P.M., when the woods are empty of hunters. This allows you to hunt the important midday period and evening. Your stand needs to be far enough from where deer bed so that you will not alert them to your presence on your approach, yet still in an area in which the deer will travel during the day. You have to be in an area that is close to bedding and has enough cover that the deer feel safe, such as a funnel between bedding areas or along the inside corner or back edge of a cornfield.

Another way to use hunters' typical patterns to your advantage is to get to your stand extremely early. Again, you have to use an access route that allows you to get to your stand without spooking any deer. In the morning, never enter your stand through crops (standing corn is perhaps an exception); you should enter though the woods. By being in place at least an hour before daylight, you will be in position to intercept any deer that other hunters may spook ahead of them by their un-thought-through approach as dawn is breaking. The deer will casually flee ahead of the approaching hunter and could possibly spend the first few minutes of light casually milling about the edge of thick cover. This is, of course, where you should be set up.

Figure out the habits of the other hunters in your area, pattern them, and determine how the deer react to this pattern. Make no mistake about it, deer generally have the hunters patterned much better than the other way around.

CHAPTER 8

Nocturnal Bucks

The nocturnal buck has become almost a mythical creature in a lot of areas, often thought of as nearly unkillable. The key words here are "almost" and "nearly." No deer is completely nocturnal, and not even the oldest, most experienced buck stays nocturnal during the rut periods. When hunting deer that experience hunting pressure, nearly all bucks become what most hunters refer to as "nocturnal" by the time they reach the age of three and a half to four and a half years, and in extremely pressured areas by the time they reach the age of two and a half. This means that the bucks make nearly 100 percent of their movements between just after dark and just before daylight. All deer, though, do move during daylight hours, even if it's just to stand up, take a few steps, and bed back down in the same spot. Once a buck reaches this stage, it's almost impossible to kill him until the prerut or rut. I don't believe there is such a thing as an unkillable buck. I do believe, however, that with average hunting methods, you are relying more on luck than anything else.

Some average hunting habits are, for example, arriving at your tree ten minutes before first light or leaving your stand between 9:00 and 10:00 A.M. during the rut periods. There are several others, such as arriving for an evening hunt as little as two hours before dark during the rut periods, or hunting the same few stands frequently during the early part of the season when the weather is nice, and then not very often once it starts to get cold during the rut phases. Another is fair-weather hunting—not going out when you know you're going to get wet or be uncomfortable due to unpleasant weather. Yet another average hunting habit is hunting the first good sign you come across without knowing the entire layout of the property you're hunting. These average hunting methods are fine if you are out for a bit of recreation, but if you are seriously hunting for a mature buck, you have to change your habits and methods.

A prime example of a nocturnal buck was one that I shot during the rut in 1997. The area in which this buck lived was littered with large buck sign for at least four years. The regular pattern to the sign indicated that it was the same buck making the sign. Despite all the sign, I had never seen the buck—that is, until late October 1995. During a heavy rainstorm, I went out to set up a tree in a new location. I knew the rain would mask my scent and the noise from cutting branches and moving them around. The area was on the backside of a large standing cornfield and had many scrapes and rubs littering it. It was definitely a primary scrape area. I finished the tree at about noon, and all I could think about was getting out of my soaked, cold clothing. Walking back around the corner of the standing cornfield, I came to an abrupt halt. There, not forty yards away, was the nocturnal buck freshening a scrape in the still pouring rain. He had ten typical points with unmistakable large, forked brow tines and sported about an eighteen- to twenty-inch inside spread. Within seconds, he noticed me standing there. We stared at each other for what seemed like minutes, but in reality it was probably not more than ten seconds. I thought he would bound into the standing corn, a mere two or three yards away, but instead he turned and ran through the fifteen-yard buffer of weeds into the woods.

I had seven stand locations in that woods and along that cornfield, one of them within ten yards of the runway he took into the woods, and in three years of hunting that property I had never before seen that buck. All my stands had also been set up since March of that year, so the thought that he might have altered his pattern because of my preseason scouting was out of the question. That year I had hunted the wooded area only half a dozen times, so the area was not getting overhunted. There were two other bowhunters on the property, but I did not know how often they hunted. I did know, however, that they hunted the same two perimeter stands all the time, and that those stands were not along the cornfield. I hunted for this buck the remainder of the 1995 and all of the 1996 season without seeing him even once, despite the fact that he left obvious sign in the same places each year.

On November 4, 1997, the weather forecast called for an all-day light rain on the fifth, so I decided to sit all day along a rub and scrape line in the same woods where the large buck was presumably still living. All his sign was still showing up in the same places and in the same manner. After sitting from an hour and a half before first light until almost dark without seeing any deer, I had a doe sneak through at a distance of about thirty yards in some heavy brush. Not far behind her was the nocturnal buck. It was the first time I had seen him in over two years. He moved through the brush rapidly, pursuing the doe, and did not offer a shot, but I could not help but notice the many points and large, forked brow tines. The buck had started to decline, and he had a much narrower inside spread and shorter tines than when I first saw him two years earlier.

November 11, 1997, was my next trip back to that area. It was a cold, crisp, overcast morning. Hanging in my sling, I watched several does and twin six-points meander through the tight funnel of heavy cover that connected the woodlot to a large marsh. At 10:00 A.M., it started to snow very heavily. By 10:30, the snow stopped, leaving about an inch on the ground. At 10:45, another bowhunter walked right under the tree I was in. After getting his attention and finding out he did not have permission, I asked him to leave. Watching him leave his footprints in the moist snow with his breathable leather boots, all I could think of was the scent he was leaving behind. If a mature buck came in, I would have to take my shot before he crossed the hunter's tracks. Moist snow holds scent extremely well, as any rabbit hunter who hunts behind dogs can tell you.

Though disappointed that a hunter had just walked through and left his scent on the ground, I decided to stick with my original plan and remain in my tree until noon. At 11:30, I noticed a large deer moving toward me through the brush about sixty yards away. Even though the wind was swirling in all directions, my Scent-Lok suit worked as designed, and the deer progressed steadily. At fifty yards, the deer passed through a small opening, and I immediately recognized it as the nocturnal buck that had eluded me the previous three seasons. As he slipped through the brush, I admired the many points, mass, and large, forked brow tines that made this buck so unmistakable. He was closing fast and soon was within twenty yards. His course would take him through the shooting lane where the other hunter had walked less than an hour earlier. As his nose was clearing the edge of the brush, I came to full draw. The instant his chest was exposed, I vocally bleatted to stop his determined pace. He halted just a few steps before reaching the bootprints in the snow. He was now a mere ten yards away from me, standing broadside. I opened my fingers and watched my arrow disappear just behind his shoulder. In an instant flash of survival instinct, he bolted fifty yards before he fell, struggled to get back up, fell again, and expired.

It was the fourth season I had hunted for this particular buck. In those four seasons, I only saw him three times: twice while on stand and once while scouting. My first encounter with him was during a driving rainstorm, the second also while it was raining on a day during the early part of the rut, and the third just after a powerful midday snow squall. This was a so-called "nocturnal" buck living in a highly pressured area, and he

I saw this fourteen-point nocturnal buck only three times in four seasons before taking him in 1997.

only moved during daylight hours under certain circumstances in which he felt safe. This 150-class fourteen-point had an inside spread of just under twelve inches and was definitely in his declining years, which was also obvious by his severely worn teeth.

The first opportunity to take a nocturnal buck is while he is still in his summer routine, before he becomes nocturnal. Bucks usually become nocturnal after their core area has been intruded upon, often by hunters scouting. If a hunter has the opportunity to watch the summer pattern of a mature buck, he should have an excellent opportunity to kill that buck on the first or second day of the season. Mature bucks in their summer patterns are very vulnerable before any scouting or hunting pressure. You will be catching the buck totally off guard if you set up where you have been regularly seeing him enter or exit a field or woodlot. Make sure you prepare the location as quickly and as scent-free as possible. The area should then be totally left alone until you hunt it. Any human activity prior to season will lower your chances of taking that buck during the first day or two. If you hunt this spot a couple times without any luck, back off and leave the area alone.

After the first few days of season, things change dramatically. The mature bucks will seem to have vanished, and you must change your tactics accordingly. Two keys to have any chance at consistently tagging nocturnal bucks in pressured areas are patience and discipline. Being patient, and not hunting your best stands until the prerut starts, is critical to consistent success. You must also be disciplined, especially on morning hunts, and be in your stand and settled in early, very early, sometimes an hour and a half before daylight during the rut periods. Two hours is even better in certain situations, such as hunting in a staging area or primary scrape area. This is especially important when the staging area or primary scrape area is located near a feeding area, and even more so during the various rut stages. This may seem like a long time to sit in the dark, and it is, but the results can definitely be worth the wait. I often doze in my sling, with one ear open, until daylight. You may be wondering why in the world I would sit there so long just to have the buck I'm after walk past in the dark. The answer is found in pressured mature buck behavior, which took me decades of mistakes to unravel.

Prior to the rut phases, pressured mature bucks will leave their night-time feeding areas before daylight and return to their bedding areas for the day. That is why these bucks are almost impossible to kill before the rut. Unless you are sitting within shooting distance of a buck's bed, you probably won't have a chance. By the time it's light enough to shoot, that's where he will already be. If you decide to take the chance and hunt within shooting distance of where you think a specific mature buck's bedding location is, it will more than likely be a one-time deal. If he doesn't happen to come within shooting distance, you'll more than likely spook him when you leave the area, which could very well alter where he beds from then on. This will also alert the buck to your presence, perhaps making him even more cautious. So when hunting a nocturnal buck, you will be doing yourself a favor by totally avoiding his core bedding zone until the prerut arrives.

If a hunter approaches a mature buck's transition zone just before first light while the buck is present, this will cause the buck to alter the timing of his daily return to his bedding area, arriving even earlier than before, in essence staying one step ahead of the hunter. The only way to solve this problem is to get there first. While hunting for nocturnal bucks, I sometimes get to my stand as early as three hours before first light, especially during rut periods. If you are there first, you will not spook the buck while you walk to your tree, and there's a chance you will get an opportunity to see your nocturnal buck as he takes a few minutes to cruise the last few yards into his bedding area at first light. If you sit until 2 P.M. during the rut stages, there's also a good chance that the buck will come out of his bedding area late in the morning to scent-check for does that may have passed through after daylight.

The second, and equally important, aspect of hunting nocturnal bucks is just as time-consuming: Stay late. You are hunting mature bucks conditioned to heavy hunting pressure. In many areas, these bucks have been hunted and have had experience with hunters since they were fawns. They know when hunters arrive and leave. Most hunters leave the woods around 9:00 or 10:00 A.M. Mature bucks are aware of and conditioned to the normal hunter time frame. Quite often in heavily hunted areas, bucks will simply wait for hunters to leave before getting on with their daily routine. More important, though, is that all mature bucks have a natural daily rhythm that includes a pattern of movement at midday, especially during the rut stages.

During the prerut, a mature buck leaves his nightly route before the does. He beds down for a few hours until late morning or midday, at which time he rises and cruises the edges of bedding areas, scent-checking for estrous does. If he crosses the path of an estrous doe, he will follow, but if not, he will travel through the best available cover from bedding area to bedding area within his core area. A buck that arrived in his bedding area unspooked will often rise and do his scent-checking between 10:00 A.M. and 2:00 P.M. During this time of day during the rut stages, I've seen more mature bucks than at any other time. It follows that a good procedure is to get to your tree very early and stay late. This requires a great deal of discipline and will often mean long hours on stand without seeing any deer. Not seeing deer can be frustrating, but that mystical "nocturnal" buck could be your reward while other hunters are at home having lunch.

Just as important as daily timing in the pursuit of mature bucks is seasonal timing. Mature bucks are, generally speaking, more nocturnal throughout the entire year than the rest of the herd. One thing that saves the lives of many mature bucks every fall is that when cover becomes scarce, big bucks tend to become even more nocturnal. When the leaves begin to fall, a lot of places where the buck has been secure throughout the entire summer turn bare and open. Mature bucks feel uncomfortable in this changing environment and react by moving only under the cover of darkness. This is great for the bucks and terrible for the hunters. A buck's natural rhythm allows him to pinpoint hunter activity after dark. He may pass through the area and notice the scent you've left behind, hear you enter or exit your stand when you hunt close to bedding areas, or take note of other deer that have been spooked by your presence. He will then avoid the area or move through it only after dark.

It is not until the prerut that sexual urges force mature bucks out of their nocturnal ways and into moving during daylight. This does not mean that a mature buck will just start walking around before dark. It simply means he is more likely to move during the day if hunting pressure has not changed the daytime doe activity. If you over hunt your best stands during the time when mature bucks are most nocturnal, the middle three weeks of October in my home state, you are potentially ruining your chances at killing any mature buck in the area for the remainder of the season. Not altering regular movements of deer prior to the rut is critical for success during it.

You can counter this situation by waiting to hunt your best stands until the prerut. The prerut usually begins around the last week of October in the North and as late as mid to late December in the South, so you have to know when it occurs where you are hunting. By waiting for this period, you will avoid contaminating the area with your scent too early in the season, so that when it arrives, the deer will move in an undisturbed manner. During the prerut, you have the best chance at a mature nocturnal buck. Timing is everything!

I took the top one thousand typical whitetails listed in the twenty-second recording period statistical summary book of the Pope and Young Club and divided them up according to the month they were taken. Here are the results in percentages: September, 6 percent; October, 29 percent; November, 56 percent; December, 7 percent; January, 2 percent.

This shows that even though many states have a large portion of the month of November designated for gun season, it still dominates as the most productive month for record-book bucks by bowhunters. These numbers also reinforce the fact that most mature bucks are taken during the rut stages.

When I think of nocturnal bucks becoming vulnerable during the rut stages, I immediately think of a buck that became known to all of my hunting buddies as "the Wheezer." Due to his unbelievable social habits with several matriarch does, along with his uncanny ability to exit an area without making a sound, and the fact that he was extremely nocturnal, this buck was very difficult to hunt. In all my years of hunting, I have never encountered a buck even close to being as smart, careful, and lucky as the Wheezer.

My first encounter with the Wheezer was in October 1997, while hunting out of a large oak. Under a lone tree fifteen yards away and next to a standing cornfield was a primary scrape area. Just at daylight, I decided to do a couple rattling sequences. The first sequence was all it took. A very respectable eight-point stepped out of the corn and offered me a ten-yard broadside shot. As my cams rolled over while drawing my bow, one of the plastic draw length elements made a previously unnoticeable tick against the aluminum cam. The buck heard this and immediately bolted a short distance, stopping just out of my range. I did not realize at the time how much frustration that two-and-a-half-year-old eight-point was going to cause me over the next three seasons.

On October 2, 1998, a friend of mine who hunts the same farm rattled in the same buck out of the same tree just before dark. He had a decoy set up, which probably cost him a shot. The buck and a mature doe crossed the ditch from a bedding area into what was that year a soybean field. The doe walked toward the decoy as the buck stood along the edge of the field about fifty yards away. Does tend to figure out that decoys are not real much quicker than bucks. She soon spooked, taking the buck with her. Now, as a three-and-a-half-year-old, he had grown to about a sixteen-inch-wide heavy-antlered eight-point.

Later that same season, while on an evening hunt during the prerut, I had my second encounter with this buck. Hunting from the same oak tree where both of the previous encounters had occurred, I had him walking directly toward me through a large weed field. Between my tree and the weed field is a muddy eight-yard-wide ditch and then a ten-yard-wide grassy buffer to a patch of red brush, which runs about twenty yards out into the tall weeds. This weed field had become this buck's core area. The oak is situated right on the edge of the ditch and five yards from the edge of the cropfield. The buck entered the red brush and stopped just short of the grassy buffer; another step would have given me a twenty-yard shot. What happened next not only amazed me, but it also gave him his name.

The buck stood there like a rock until it was just about dark, and then he wheezed. I have heard bucks wheeze a couple times before, but this was definitely different. Bucks usually wheeze when there are other bucks around, as a sign of dominance. Within seconds of his wheezing, three large does that were feeding in the beanfield trotted across the field, crossed the ditch within twenty yards of me, and started scent-checking the grassy buffer. They remained there for about twenty minutes. I could hear them taking in air through their nostrils in an attempt to detect any danger. It reminded me of bodyguards checking to see if it was safe, for the man in charge to pass through. They never approached the buck, but walked by him several times as if this were routine. Being satisfied that it was safe, the does eventually crossed back to the other side of the ditch. Unfortunately, by then it was dark. My activated Scent-Lok suit and rubber boots had kept the does from winding me or smelling where I had walked to my tree.

I never heard the buck leave the brush. I waited for about an hour and a half after dark before exiting my tree so that I would not spook him if he were still close by. He had departed without making a sound. All the way back to my vehicle, I kept thinking about how unusual the deer behavior was that I had just witnessed, and that nobody would believe me. I really did not care if anyone believed me, but I was excited to have the opportunity to hunt such a buck. From this moment on, we began to call this buck the Wheezer.

Neither I nor anyone else I know ever saw the Wheezer again that season. I thought about the Wheezer a lot the next summer, and whether or not he made it through gun season. The area where the Wheezer lived receives a lot of both gun- and bowhunting pressure. Fortunately, most of the large weed field, which was his core area, is property that does not get hunted. The farmer rotated the cropfield into corn in 1999. On October 1, I was walking down the edge of the corn toward my tree an hour and a half before daybreak, when the sounds of bucks sparring across the ditch in the weed field caught my attention. Could it be that my extra-early entry on opening day to guarantee I would not spook any deer was not early enough? As the bucks kept sparring about seventy yards away, I quietly climbed into my Ambush Sling twenty-five feet up my oak. The bucks kept sparring and taking breaks until daylight arrived. As my eyes adjusted to the light, I could make out the Wheezer sparring with two smaller bucks. About twenty minutes after daybreak, the Wheezer stopped and let out a long, loud wheeze, and the two subordinate bucks immediately started back across the ditch and into the standing corn. One of them, a small eight-point, passed directly under my tree. The Wheezer slowly walked away and disappeared into the tall weeds. The Wheezer, now four and a half years old, was still an eight-point, but he had grown a bit larger. He now had a rack with about an eighteen-inch inside spread. I was elated to see he was still alive, but it was a little depressing to know how nocturnal he was outside of his bedding area.

Being a firm believer in not overhunting a good location, I only hunt my best stands a few times a year. I was back in my oak along the ditch for only the third time of the 1999 season. It was early November, an evening hunt, and it was a carbon copy of the evening hunt in 1998. The Wheezer came out of the tall weeds and into the red brush and wheezed. Two does stepped out of the standing corn, crossed the ditch, and scent-checked until it was dark. It was well after dark before I could leave my tree, and once again I had nothing but frustration to drag out of the woods. That was my last hunt for him that season.

Hunting season 2000 arrived, and I hoped the Wheezer had made it again. So far I had not been a worthy opponent for this wily old buck. Although I had his core area and movements clearly patterned, he was always one step ahead of me. The farmer planted corn again, which made for better hunting from my oak due to the easy and safe transition from cover to cover. At this spot, deer could move from bedding to safe feeding area in a matter of steps. At 4:30 A.M. on October 1, as I was approaching my oak tree, I spooked two deer standing beneath the annual primary scrape tree. All I could do was sigh as my flashlight beam crossed paths with the Wheezer as he splashed across the ditch, hightailing it for the weed field. Yeah, he made it another season, but it was two and a half hours before daylight, and he was making a scrape before crossing into his bedding area for the day. I climbed into my sling to hunt the remainder of the morning without a chance in the world at the Wheezer. That evening I passed up a two-and-a-half-year-old eight-point while awaiting another encounter with him; however, it never happened. One thing I could not figure out was why he continued bedding in the weed field when there were at least a hundred acres of standing corn to bed in with total security. This puzzled me, because usually that much standing corn attracts the local dominant buck as a core bedding area.

On an evening hunt on October 21, I decided to try to rattle him in again. Not having rattled in that location in two seasons, I thought it might work. As the sun was dipping beneath the horizon, I started my routine. Within minutes, a deer was moving through the standing corn in my direction, so I tied my rattle bag onto my bow rope and lowered it to the ground. I jiggled it in the leaves to give the deer the exact location as he was closing in on me. As he stepped out of the corn, it was clear that this was not the Wheezer. It was a cute little six-point. After about five minutes of not seeing, hearing, or smelling anything, he slipped back into the cornfield.

It was getting dark, and I was preparing to leave my tree, when I heard a deer moving toward me down the ditch line. Could it be? Absolutely! The Wheezer was walking down the other side of the ditch toward me. I wondered whether there would be enough light by the time he got there. This turned out not to matter. The Wheezer stopped and wheezed. Two does walked out of the corn, crossed the ditch, and again started scent-checking. As one of the does started back across the ditch, I remembered my rattle bag was still on the ground. It was too late to raise it back up, and as she passed by my tree, she winded it. She snorted, and that was the end of that. It was dark by the time she snorted, but I was still disappointed in myself. I hate to have a mature animal know of my presence.

After nearly four years of specifically targeting this buck, the reality of ever taking the Wheezer was becoming very bleak. How could a buck that was so easy to pattern to a specific location be so hard to kill? The reason was obvious: He never entered my kill zone during daylight hours, at least not on the days I hunted there. I also was certain that if I hunted that oak more than three or four times per season, the Wheezer would find another entry point into the crops. There were way too many adult deer crossing that ditch in the evening for me to hunt that spot with any more regularity.

Finally, on November 3, I was perched in my oak at 3:15 P.M. That evening was extremely windy. It was so windy that I almost chose to hunt from another tree. The wind, however, turned out to be a blessing in disguise. Once in my tree, I could not help but notice the five fresh scrapes under the Wheezer's primary scrape tree. The dirt was not yet dry, so I knew they had been freshened in the last few hours. At 4:40 the Wheezer stepped out the end of the red brush at a distance of only forty yards. I was so surprised to see him that I had to pinch myself to make sure this was not a daydream. As he was moving toward the ditch, I drew my bow. I had anticipated this moment for so long that I had a momentary lapse and actually thought about taking the very poor shot. Fortunately, I regained my composure and let back down. The scrapes were fresh, and I figured he would cross the ditch to check them, eventually giving me a fifteen-yard shot.

He quietly crossed through the two-foot-deep mud ditch and circled downwind of his scrapes, which also put him directly downwind of me. I have total confidence in my Scent-Lok suit, but the thought of him winding me still crept into my thoughts. He stopped momentarily fifteen yards from his scrapes and stuck his snout in the air to scent-check them. He then dropped his head and slowly started walking toward the standing corn. It was now or never! I had waited four long years for this shot. He was just over thirty yards quartering slightly away as I drew my bow and bleatted to stop his forward progress. I had not taken a shot at that distance at a deer in over twenty years, which made me feel a little apprehensive. I placed my thirty-five-yard pin behind his shoulder and let fly. As my arrow disappeared into his chest, he wheeled and plowed back across the ditch into the security of the tall weeds. After covering sixty yards, he disappeared headlong into the weeds, never to move again.

As I walked up to the Wheezer, lying motionless in the tall weeds, I felt great respect mixed with a twinge of remorse for this wise old buck. Over several years, we had become acquainted as predator and prey. We had matched wits, and now our serious struggle had come to an end. During my bowhunting years, I've taken several bucks that I had hunted for several seasons. But never have I hunted a buck as social or worldly wise as the Wheezer. And he had several reasons to be nocturnal and

The Wheezer was taken in November 2000 after totally frustrating me for four seasons.

cautious. Upon skinning him, I discovered a twelve-gauge slug in his right hind quarter, two buckshot pellets in his neck, and a two-and-a-half-inch broadhead with two inches of aluminum shaft buried in his left shoulder. The arrow had entered above his right shoulder just below the spine and passed through the tenderloin, and then clipped the top of his left lung and buried into his left shoulder. I am quite certain that whoever took that shot assumed they had killed him. The broadhead was covered with cartilage, and the wound was at least one year old. These wounds show just how much hunting pressure there is in the area the Wheezer called home. He had eight points, an eighteen-inch inside spread, and a dressed weight of 178 pounds.

What I hope this illustrates is that hunting nocturnal bucks can take time. I hunted this buck for four years and saw him only a handful of times. The tactics I have described will work, but you have to be disciplined and not expect to have success immediately. One might wonder why, if there is that much pressure, bucks like this are living beyond gun season and reaching the ripe old age of six and a half years old or older. The answer is simple: In areas with extreme pressure, be it gun or bow,

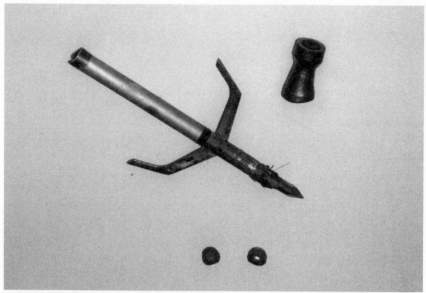

Projectiles removed from the Wheezer: buckshot, twelve-gauge slug, and two-and-a-half-inch cut broadhead.

once a buck lives beyond two and a half years, he becomes extremely difficult to see and even more difficult to kill. These old bucks are forced into having their own movement patterns, which differ greatly and are sometimes totally opposite from other deer movement patterns and time frames in the same area. And because most hunters never even get a glimpse of these bucks, they do not realize they exist. In pressured areas, these bucks must be hunted in a different manner and with more patience than the norm. While hunting mature pressured nocturnal bucks, patience is definitely a virtue.

CHAPTER 9

Hunting Scrapes

As is everything in the pursuit of whitetails, hunting over scrapes is a controversial subject. Some bowhunters think it's a waste of time. Others get very excited when they see a fresh scrape and think a big buck is going to come prancing in the first time they hunt it. A scrape is neither a waste of time nor a guarantee of success. In order to be successful, before deciding whether to hunt a scrape, you must evaluate the time of season, the location, and the quantity of scrapes and other sign in the immediate area.

A scrape is an area of ground, ranging from one to six feet in diameter, in which a buck or bucks have cleared all the leaves, grass, and weeds down to bare dirt. A scrape also has one or more licking branches above it. Although scrapes are not totally understood, I believe they are made for several reasons: as territory or dominance markers, out of simple frustration, as a year-round source of communication, and as focal points for does coming into estrus. The overhanging licking branches are the most important part of a scrape. These are used by does as well as bucks for social reasons. If you find a scrape with several recently used licking branches, you'll know it is definitely being revisited.

Scrapes can be found from September through January. The challenge to hunting over scrapes is knowing exactly how, where, and, most importantly, when to hunt them. There are four main phases of scrape activity: preseason and early season, prerut, rut, and postrut. Each stage in this annual progression of scrape activity has to be hunted specifically and requires that you adjust your tactics throughout the season.

HUNTING PRESEASON AND EARLY-SEASON SCRAPES
Preseason and early-season scrapes are usually made by mature bucks with at least one breeding season behind them. When I've found scrapes

A very visible scrape and licking branch along a standing cornfield.

in September, there usually have been sightings of a three-and-a-half-year-old or older buck in the immediate area. Scrapes made this early in the season are rare and are generally found around perimeters of food sources or bedding areas that matriarch does frequent or pass by regularly.

Early-season scrapes are usually located in perennial spots and have several licking branches over them that are used year-round by mature deer. There is no regularity to the use of these scrapes. If a scrape is located in some cover, your chances of success there might be relatively good during the first few days of season. If your preseason scouting was done properly, the bucks should still be in their summer pattern and should continue to move during daylight hours. Whitetail patterns are very consistent at this time of year, before there is any hunting pressure, so there's a good chance the buck that made the scrape will pass through the area, even if he does not pay any attention to his scrape.

After a couple days of hunting season in pressured areas, most of the scrape activity by mature bucks will be primarily after dark. In heavily hunted areas, human presence will make the three weeks of mid-October very difficult to hunt successfully, especially if you are after dominant bucks three and a half years old or older. During this period, I try to stay out of any areas that I know are going to heat up during prerut. Hunting small parcels of property on a regular basis during this three-week period can ruin any future chances of taking a mature buck. The mature bucks will be moving nocturnally, and their senses of smell and hearing will let them know of your daytime presence and after-dark departures. They will then adjust their movements around your small parcel or stand. Spooking does during this time will also alter their movements. When the mature bucks start following the does, they too will avoid your hunting location. No matter how you look at it, hunting a potential hot prerut location during the October lull will be counterproductive.

If you are scouting or finalizing your stand locations during midday in late September, look for rub lines along runways between bedding and feeding areas or large quantities of rubs in a small area. These locations are excellent setup spots for the first couple days of season, when bucks are still following their daily summer routine. If you are hunting near a dense bedding area, remember that this area is to the deer like your house is to you. There are only so many doors (runways) in or out but unlimited directions to go once outside. Any time there are rubs, scrapes, or large tracks on a runway leading into a bedding area, you can almost be certain that this is the entry or exit location a mature buck is using. Setting up quietly near that location can pay big dividends.

HUNTING PRERUT SCRAPES

My definition of prerut is the week or two just prior to the main rut. This period generally runs from October 25 through November 5 in the northern states, and as late as the second half of December in some southern states, but varies slightly from year to year depending on the weather.

Scrapes become very frequent sights during this time of the season. Bucks' testosterone levels are high, but the does are not in estrus yet; therefore, small trees and the ground take the punishment of the mature bucks' breeding aggression and sign posting. Even one-and-a-half-year-old bucks try to get involved in the breeding process by this time and are frequently seen chasing does, whether the does are in estrus or not.

Perennial primary scrape areas become extremely active at this time, but may be hard to find because most hunting areas do not offer the high-traffic, covered spots typical of primary scrape locations. A primary scrape area consists of several scrapes around a single tree, in a small area of sparse trees, or both. Primary scrapes always have several worked licking branches over them and are a major focal point of deer social behavior during the entire breeding season. Subordinate and other mature bucks frequent and use these areas, as does the dominant buck that probably started the largest scrape. Matriarch and other breeding does also use the licking branches over these scrapes when they get close to their estrous cycle.

I get excited just thinking about this time of season. The short prerut period is simply the best time to hunt in pressured areas, and anywhere else, for that matter. At this time, I pay little attention to boundary or perimeter scrapes (even though there may be many) around open fields, because they are not frequented enough during daylight hours to warrant a hunt. Now is the time to hunt those hard-to-find primary scrape areas. It is only common sense that the more scrapes there are in a primary scrape area, the more likely it is to get revisited on a regular basis. The size of the scrapes also has something to do with the amount of use they receive. Generally speaking, these areas will have one to three scrapes in them that are much wider and deeper than the rest, which means they are being used the most. When the dominant buck checks his area, he usually works the larger scrapes. The smaller scrapes in the area are less likely to be worked. This should be kept in mind when picking a tree to hunt from.

I am amazed when I read articles in which the author says that hunting scrapes is not productive. This tells me that he has never figured out how and when to hunt them properly, or he is hunting single scrapes, which are very inconsistent to hunt over. Hunting over active scrape areas during the prerut phase is as good as it gets when hunting pressured mature bucks. Finding one of these can be a huge shortcut to taking a big mature buck if hunted properly. They are generally located near feeding areas or food-bearing trees, such as apples, oaks, or chokecherries; along perimeters of bedding areas; and in funnels. During dry seasons, small water holes are also prime targets for heavy scrape activity. In general, primary scrape areas are found in the highest-traffic areas that offer some cover. In heavily hunted areas, if primary scrape areas do not offer perimeter cover from open areas, they will be used almost exclusively after dark. During my out-of-state hunts in nonpressured areas, the mature bucks visited their field edge scrapes during daylight hours. This just does not happen with any regularity in pressured areas.

Large branches twisted off over scrapes indicate that a large antlered buck is using the area. Multiple licking branches (I have seen up to twenty) over a primary scrape are visible indicators that the scrape is being revisited more frequently than is a scrape with only one or two licking branches. If you also find large-diameter rubs leading to it or around it, this just puts an additional exclamation point on the whole situation.

The best time to search for these areas is as soon as the previous hunting season is over, December or January through April. The foliage is gone, old scrapes are still easily identified, rubs stick out like sore thumbs, and you will not be contaminating the property with your presence. Primary scrape areas are almost always perennial. For best results, these areas should be found and your stands set up during postseason scouting excursions. Then, just prior to season, while wearing an activated Scent-Lok suit and odorless rubber boots, check your stand locations during midday. If you are fortunate enough to find a primary scrape area already being used, hunt it the first day or two of season, and then leave it alone until the prerut. By then the mature bucks will be on red alert, spending a lot of time (usually midday in pressured areas) looking for that first estrous female.

When you hunt a primary scrape for the first time during the prerut, hunt in the evening when the wind is in your favor. The evening entry will allow you to hunt elsewhere if there is no rut activity in the area. Walk to your stand and check the scrapes. If none is active, squirt some dominant buck urine in the largest scrape within easy shooting distance of your tree. You can also make a mock scrape, positioning it in a perfect shooting location. Make sure there is an overhanging branch, within six feet of the ground, above the spot. Scrape all the leaves out of a two-foot area with the end of a branch, being careful not to touch the end of the branch used for scraping. Then squirt some buck urine in it. The dominant buck may be enticed to start tending your scrape himself, thinking that another buck is using his scrape area. Once the area is doctored up, turn around and leave so you do not contaminate such a potential hot spot with your presence. If the scrapes are not active, the buck you are after is probably still in a nocturnal routine, and you may unknowingly tip him off to your presence if you exit after dark. Check the spot again in three or four days; during the prerut, activity levels can change rapidly.

If fresh scrapes are opened and active, hunt the spot that evening and the next morning. Hunting on consecutive visits to a hot location at this time of season is not only acceptable, it is recommended. Your best time for bagging a mature buck during the prerut when hunting a primary scrape area is between 9:00 A.M. and 2 P.M. Over the past ten years, I've taken several large bucks between 10:00 A.M. and 2 P.M., and I've seen several others during those hours that were out of range. Dominant breeding bucks scent-check their territory during this time, trying to locate does in or close to their estrous cycle that may have passed through during regular morning movement hours, which are usually from daybreak until 9:00 A.M. Mature bucks can be compared to older, mature men. They simply do not want to expend any more energy than they have to. Dominant bucks waste as little energy as possible in the pursuit of estrous does, whereas subordinate bucks will chase does even before they are close to their estrous cycle, and at any time of day.

During the prerut, mature bucks in pressured areas either bed in their regular bedding areas or stage up in good cover near heavy traffic areas well before first light. They then wait until late in the morning, after most of the deer have passed through, to scent-check their territories. During the prerut, they check the bedding areas, funnels, and scrape areas in their core areas, and if nothing interests their noses, they then bed down. It has always amazed me how many big bucks are taken in the middle of the day during gun season. Even veteran hunters often attribute this fact to other hunters moving the deer around as they head to lunch or simply get up to take a walk. In some cases that is indeed true, but for the most part it has nothing to do with it. The mature bucks are simply following their normal midday routine for that time of the season.

When hunting a primary scrape area in the morning, it is critical to arrive early. You must be set up and quiet so as not to spook deer passing through prior to daybreak. Be in your stand and settled a minimum of one to one and a half hours before dawn, entering in such a fashion that you do not spook deer that may be feeding in the vicinity. There is an excellent chance the dominant buck will pass by and freshen his scrapes a half hour to an hour before first light, and you must be set up so that he may pass by unalarmed. Later in the morning, after all the other deer have moved through, he may return to check his core area, including his primary scrapes. If he was spooked by your entry, he will not return later in the morning. There is also a chance he will stage up within hearing distance of the area prior to first light and wait for a doe to pass through after daylight. These does could entice him to get up, exit his bed, check them for receptivity, and possibly present a shot opportunity. Mornings have always been my preference when hunting an active primary scrape area, mainly because deer seem to be more at ease in the morning after moving all night undisturbed. Do not leave your stand until at least 2:00 P.M.; if possible, stay all day. Pressured mature bucks must use a different time schedule than their nonpressured brethren in order to survive.

Hunts over a primary scrape area should be repeated at least every two or three days, as long as the scrapes are active. Be extremely careful not to spook deer with your entry and exit. An active scrape area during the prerut has a short window of opportunity that must be taken advantage of. Try not to hunt close to the area during other hunts unless there is a rub line or scrape line leading to it. It is very possible during an evening hunt that you might intercept a buck on one of these rub lines prior to his reaching the primary scrape area after dark. A line of active scrapes along a travel route is definitely worth hunting a couple times. Individual single scrapes, not in any pattern, more than likely will not be revisited and should not be hunted. During this short, very critical time of the season, you should always have a reason for hunting where you are hunting and for using whatever tactics you may be using. Hunting without a plan during the prerut period will definitely lead to inconsistent results.

Rattling or grunting can be very effective when hunting a primary scrape area during the prerut and rut, if done properly and in moderation. This is also the time to consider using a decoy if you are hunting in an open area. If the situation is right, a combination of tactics could be deadly. Before you attempt to rattle or use a decoy, your first two hunts in an active scrape area should allow the deer to move as they normally would. The best shot opportunities always come when a buck is caught totally by surprise and comes into the scrape area on his own. Any time you use a tactic—any type of calling, rattling, or a decoy—to bring in a mature buck, he will be much more aware of his surroundings, thus making it more difficult to get off a shot.

A good example of a successful prerut primary scrape hunt was one that took place in early November 1996. The primary scrape area was located about twenty yards from the corner of a large field of weeds, inside a small, forty-yard-wide neck of woods with sparse cover, and was surrounded on three sides by an extremely thick and large bedding area. This spot was a corridor of heavy deer traffic. There were many runways, scrapes, and rubs throughout the small zone. The first evening I hunted there, I saw a pack of coyotes and a small six-point. I momentarily considered shooting the alpha male of the coyote pack as he chewed on an old bone not fifteen yards from my tree. Knowing that if I shot him I would have to make noise recovering him and leave his scent in the area, I decided to stick to deer hunting. After hunting the next morning in a different area, I returned to the primary scrape area for another evening hunt. Several does had already passed through, when a single doe trotted by panting. Immediately I moved into position for a shot along her back trail. Within a minute, a nice buck appeared, nose glued to the ground, following her exact steps. I drew my bow and waited until he was broadside at a distance of only eighteen yards. I then bleated to stop him. At the instant he stopped, I released my arrow. The nine-point collapsed after running only forty yards.

Primary scrape areas during the prerut have, without question, been my most consistent locations for taking mature bucks. The bucks are coming out of their nocturnal patterns at this time, keeping a routine, checking their scrapes, and looking for estrous does prior to the rut. This is the time of year when your chances of taking a mature buck are greatest.

HUNTING RUT SCRAPES

The main rut begins when does start coming into estrus. Testosterone levels in bucks are at their peak. Mature bucks search for does in estrus and stay with them during their short breeding cycles, then search for another. This means their daily movements and general patterns can be unpredictable and take them a long way from their core area. There will still be some scrape activity, but this scraping will be more coincidental than determined. Scrape activity by mature bucks slows down drastically during this rut period, which in the northern states starts in early November and continues through the month. In some southern states, the rut does not start until mid-December or January.

During the main rut, scrape hunting becomes very hit or miss, with no regularity to anything. Primary scrape areas may go unnoticed during this time by the dominant buck that started them. They may remain somewhat active, however, in areas with high buck-to-doe ratios and will be frequented by other mature and subordinate bucks due to their location in high-traffic transition zones.

As the mature breeding does come into estrus, they lead the dominant males around on very unpredictable routes. The mature bucks chase and follow these does no matter where they go. Mature bucks will, however, try to steer does into areas with adequate cover for breeding purposes. Unfortunately for them, the does do not always cooperate. This lack of cooperation on the does' part and almost total lack of caution from the bucks is why many big bucks get killed by cars during the rut. I once had to stop my car to allow a very large ten-point to cross in front of it. He never took his nose off the ground to look up at me. This was because he was scent-trailing a doe in heat. This behavior also helps balance the scale for all hunters. During this period, luck plays almost as big a part as skill. It's a great time to be in the woods, because there's always the chance of something happening, even if you are doing everything wrong.

During the rut, sit in high-traffic areas and make sure you don't spook the mature does, which are like buck magnets. Hunting over a primary scrape area can still be productive, as they are in high-traffic areas and get visited by does coming into estrus. There is a good chance of sighting a big buck that moved in from another area while pursuing estrous does. At this time, you cannot count on a mature buck following any pattern as you could during the prerut.

HUNTING POSTRUT SCRAPES

Postrut is the period after the first main rut phase and preceding the second, lower-key rut phase. In pressured areas, scrape activity will depend on how many and which bucks remain alive after gun season, as well as how much stress due to hunting pressure was put on them. That pressure will also influence whether the scrapes, if any, are being made nocturnally. Indeed, most scrape activity is nocturnal. Even in areas with minimal hunting pressure, scrape activity during this period will be greatly reduced from the prerut activity level.

By early December in northern states, and as late as January in some southern states, scrapes will start being used again if a mature buck still inhabits the area. Some early fawns and does that did not get bred the first time around will come into estrus again, creating a much lower-profile second rut. I recently read an article by a noted author who wrote that there is no such thing as a second rut. This is simply not true. That single article told me that the author hunts extremely nonpressured areas where the buck-to-doe ratios are relatively even. In areas like those, every doe that comes into estrus is going to get bred during her first cycle. In pressured areas, where the buck-to-doe ratios are always extremely lopsided in the does' favor, there are does that do not get bred during their first estrous cycle. There simply are not enough bucks to get the job done so expediently. There are also early doe fawns that will come into estrus in December. Throw in the fact that 70 to 80 percent of the buck population gets killed during the first two days of gun season in these already out-of-balance deer herds, and it's easy to see that the odds of does being bred during their first cycle become even lower. Hunters who hunt in areas where there is no obvious second rut should feel very fortunate that they are not hunting in a pressured area.

Highly pressured areas will have little to no daytime movement by dominant bucks after gun season. If there is daytime movement, it will probably take place during midday, just as during the prerut. In the northern regions, December often brings snow, which will leave ample sign of everything that's going on. Hunt a bit higher, and look for trees with some background cover. The added height will help keep you out of the deer's peripheral vision, and the background cover will keep you from sticking out like a sore thumb against the skyline. Deer start feeding heavily with the coming of winter, and their travel routes become very routine. They start to group up at this time and travel together, making travel routes very easy to locate.

The best way to hunt during postrut or second rut is to stick close to the well-traveled corridors between bedding and feeding areas. Also look for secondary runways with large tracks, rubs, or scrapes along them. Active scrapes along these secondary runways indicate that they are being used by a buck. By this time of year, even the year-and-a-half-old bucks have probably done some breeding and could be responsible for the scrapes. I've taken two big bucks in December that would not travel the main runs that the rest of the deer were using. Both were in heavily pressured areas and used their own secondary travel routes that offered more cover.

One of those bucks I took on December 17, 1997. While scouting a new property, I spooked a large buck that was bedded with a doe just inside the edge of a bedding area. After he disappeared into the bedding area, I went over to identify his tracks in the four inches of snow that had been on the ground for almost a week. He had nearly an inch of hoof missing in his right front track, making his route easy to identify. After moving back into the open woods that separated the bedding area from a picked cornfield, I found his tracks and followed them through the woods toward the corn. It was obvious that he was using his own separate trail; it had old rubs along it and a single small scrape that he had recently opened. The majority of the deer in the area were using two other runways that skirted each side of the woods. Accordingly, I prepped a tree along the buck's travel route and returned to hunt that evening. The hunt was relatively quiet, as I hung comfortably in my sling thirty feet off the ground. Between 4:00 and 5:00 P.M., I saw five does and fawns heading along the north side of the woods toward the cut corn. Darkness fell with no more sightings.

The mercury was at eight degrees the next morning. I arrived well before daylight so I would not spook any deer traveling the corridor just before first light. I also placed a four-point decoy near my stand. The decoy had been converted from eight points to four so that it would not intimidate younger bucks. Nothing happened until about 9:00 A.M., when nine does and fawns and a small six-point traversed the north edge of the woods, taking the same path as the night before, only in the other direction. The six-point noticed the decoy and became very inquisitive. He left his travel route and sneaked in to check things out. Once at the decoy, he slowly circled it for fifteen minutes before deciding the fake four-point would not give him the time of day. By 10:00 A.M., all the deer were safely in their bedding area, and it became very still. The edge of the bedding area was only about a hundred yards in front of me, and with all the foliage gone, I could see it perfectly.

At 10:15 A.M., the action began. Does started exploding out of their small sanctuary as if a hunter were walking through it. I knew this could not possibly be the case, because once they were outside of their bedding area, they just skirted it a little and went back in. The small six-point could not possibly be responsible for such havoc, and he wasn't. The large buck from the day before burst onto the scene and started chasing does in and out of the brush. At one point he followed a doe to within thirty-five yards of my perch. The shot he presented was not to my liking, so I waited. I thought he would take note of the decoy, but he never even looked in its direction, and I ended up without a shot. By 11:30 A.M., all deer activity had vanished back into the bedding area. I had a 1:00 P.M. appointment and had to pull my decoy and head to work, but a couple hours later I was back in my tree. That afternoon I broke one of my own rules by hunting out of the same tree three straight times. Other than during the prerut, I normally don't hunt the same tree more than twice in one week, let alone three times in a row. But I felt comfortable knowing I had not spooked any deer.

The afternoon hunt started where the morning hunt left off. At 4:00 P.M., the big buck appeared along the edge of the bedding area and started to skirt around it. He soon cut back in, and the does started to file out. This time, though, they did not go back in. They proceeded to make their way along the north edge of the woods. After watching eight does and fawns and the six-point use the trail along the woods edge, I really started to question my stand location. It was far too late for second-guessing, so all I could do was hope for the best. As 4:45 P.M. passed by, so did the last doe of the nine I had counted in the morning. It was now 5:00, and thoughts of the upcoming Christmas and New Year's festivities left me

This twelve-point, taken in December 1997, would not follow the well-traveled runways with the does after gun season.

with the realization that this would be my last opportunity to hunt for this magnificent buck.

The sound of crunching snow pulled me back from my daydreaming to the task at hand. As I carefully peeked around the tree to which my sling was attached, the big buck was already at twenty-five yards and coming closer, following his own separate route through the woods. As he stepped broadside at eight yards, I vocally halted his forward progress with a short bleat. He stopped, and I released. The arrow disappeared just above his shoulder. He spun and ran the hundred yards back to the bedding area and disappeared. The distance he covered led me to believe I had only hit one lung. After forty-five minutes, I descended my tree and slowly, very quietly, began searching for blood in the snow. After tracking for fifty yards in the noisy crunching snow without finding any blood or my arrow, I decided to leave the woods.

I had several hours to kill, so I changed my clothes and went to a restaurant for a pizza before returning to continue the search. It was a little after 8:00 P.M. when I found the buck, about a hundred yards inside the bedding area. He was in a bedded position facing his backtrack, which justified my decision to wait. The arrow had clipped the top of one lung and passed through the other, but did not exit. This explained the minimal amount of blood externally. The buck sported a wide twelve-point rack and was a worthy end to a very good season.

CHAPTER 10

Hunting Staging Areas

Understanding what staging areas are and how bucks use them is one of the most important, yet overlooked and misunderstood, aspects of hunting mature pressured whitetails. A staging area is a high-traffic pass-through area where mature bucks stage, or lie in wait for other deer to pass through during the rut stages. This staging zone allows dominant bucks to intercept possible estrous does during their normal daytime movements to and from feeding and bedding areas without exposing themselves to danger in the open. A staging area is used mostly during the short prerut period. They are, however, also used throughout all the rut periods when they are needed, if they remain undisturbed. Traditional staging areas also see some buck traffic early in the season. This is because staging areas are often relatively close to feeding areas, and bucks will enter a staging area and remain there until it is dark and safe to enter the feeding area. During the rut, when mature bucks are with estrous does, they abandon their staging areas until there is a need to use them again. If you are hunting an area with a low buck-to-doe ratio (almost all heavily hunted property falls into this category) or with high deer concentrations, a mature buck may never need to use a staging area during the main rut phase. He will have so many does to breed and so little competition that he will not have to stage up in order to find an estrous doe.

Hunters often have difficulty recognizing staging areas, but they are unmistakable if you know what to look for. A staging area looks very similar to, and sometimes also serves as, the dominant buck's primary scrape area. A staging area is littered with rubs, scrapes, and runways, and it must have some sort of cover between it and any open cropfields or open areas. Staging areas are almost always established near a break or change in the terrain. I most often find them inside corners of fields, on points, and in fingers adjacent to cropfields or other major food sources. Another excellent location is anywhere there is heavier-than-normal cover that connects a bedding area to a feeding area. Staging areas remain in the same place year after year, unless there are major habitat changes, such as property development or crop rotation. Crop rotation can alter the amount of deer traffic in a staging area from year to year by altering where the preferred food source is located.

A staging area may be as small as ten yards in diameter or it could be eighty yards long. This depends on numerous variables, such as available cover, the size of the cropfield it borders, and the number of deer passing through the area. In agricultural regions, staging areas are generally located ten to fifty yards off the primary food source being used during the prerut and rut periods. Why so close to the crops? The answer to that question is simple. This is the first place where possible estrous does can be intercepted just before or just after daylight as they are leaving the fields. Cropfields are also destination points in the evening and after dark. It's much safer and more efficient for a dominant buck to lie in wait than to wander through the woods in search of the does that will eventually pass through his staging area anyway. In pressured areas, mature bucks do not survive long in open areas.

The larger the staging area, the more difficult it is to hunt, because bucks are not confined to a small zone. It has been my experience that the smaller the staging area, the less likely it is to be visited or used by subordinate bucks in the area. Large staging areas are found where there are high concentrations of deer and are often used by several mature bucks. When the dominant buck is preoccupied with an estrous doe, other mature and subordinate bucks take advantage of his absence by using the staging area.

A piece of property that I hunt has a very long, narrow annual staging area that starts about twenty yards inside the woods and parallels a large cropfield for at least eighty yards. It passes through mature oaks and maples with scattered saplings and is bordered by a thick row of briers along the field. Although I do not hunt this staging area very often, I have to pass through it to get to a much smaller staging area about two hundred yards away, across a ditch next to another, smaller cropfield. The small area always has several scrapes around a small oak tree with low-hanging branches and several rubs on some nearby red brush. This small zone borders a large weed field that is used as a bedding area. I prefer to hunt the smaller staging area because the chances of having a buck within shooting distance are much greater. In five seasons, I've taken two good bucks from this small staging area. The larger staging area receives frequent hunting pressure from other hunters. Their constant pressure and

This buck was taken next to a small staging area that was located two hundred yards from a much larger staging area.

typical arrival time in the woods, a half hour before daylight or later, tend to push mature bucks out of the large staging area. This helps to make my little area more productive.

Staging areas are far more prevalent in agricultural areas than in big-woods areas. This is because mature bucks do not like to be exposed in open areas during daylight. A mature buck will chase an estrous doe wherever she may lead him once he finds her, but his comfort level definitely decreases once he is exposed in an open area. I've watched dominant mature bucks chasing does in open fields during the rut, and the bucks almost always attempt to cut the does off and force them toward cover. By mature bucks, I am referring to bucks three and a half years old and older. Adolescent bucks never seem to have a plan and do not seem to be concerned about chasing does in open areas. This is probably due to immaturity and the fact that they have not had many encounters with hunters at that stage in their lives. The older the buck, the more likely he is to remain within some sort of cover even while chasing does. In pressured areas, this is imperative if he is to survive. As hunting pressure increases and foliage falls from the trees, the amount of time a mature buck spends in thick cover increases.

Because there is usually some sort of cover everywhere in most big-woods areas, staging areas are not as prevalent there. Also, most heavily wooded areas do not have defined feeding destination areas like agricultural areas do. In northern wooded regions, which I hunted exclusively for fifteen years, I can remember finding staging areas only five times, and they were not used by the bucks nearly as regularly as the ones I have hunted in agricultural areas.

In big-woods regions, staging areas also are not as defined as in agricultural regions. In large wooded areas, a staging area is often simply a funnel of some sort between a feeding and bedding area. At the narrowest point of the funnel, there should be some scrapes and rubs. This is more than likely the best possible location for heavy deer traffic in the area. Bucks are aware of this and will stage at this spot to intercept estrous does.

An example of a big-woods staging area was one that I hunted twenty-five years ago. It consisted of a funnel of excellent cover at the base of a long oak ridge leading into a cedar swamp. At the base of the ridge was an area of sparse brush with many rubs and a few scrapes. Because the large oak ridge received a lot of hunting pressure, the dominant buck would move into this staging area well before first light and wait for does to pass through later in the morning. For several years during the prerut and rut, I almost always jumped a single buck bedded there while walking to my stand in the morning. During that stage of my bowhunting career, I usually arrived at my stand no earlier than a half hour before first light. And that buck was always there ahead of me. How did I know it was a buck? Something you cannot mistake about a mature buck during the rut is his odor. During the rut, mature bucks get a rather putrid musky odor from urinating on their tarsal glands, which are located on the inside of their rear legs at knee level. The large tufts of fur turn very dark brown during the rut, and the odor from the urine and bacteria is unmistakable. I will never forget the very pungent odor that filled the air when I neared the spot where that buck had been bedded. It took me several years to figure out what that buck and others were up to.

These bucks were entering their staging areas well before first light and waiting for the does to pass through after daylight. The reason was really very simple. They had been conditioned by hunting pressure to be nocturnal since early in the season. This means that they would enter the staging area during the same nocturnal time frame they had been conditioned to prior to the rut phases, which was well before first light. Their sexual urges, however, overcame their survival instincts during the prerut and rut, so instead of entering their bedding area, they lay in waiting in some form of cover for estrous does. This is why a staging area always has some type of cover around most of its perimeter. The cover serves as an escape route and also allows the buck to detect any approaching predators, primarily humans, before they spot him. Bucks usually bed down in the perimeter cover surrounding the staging area so that the wind is at their backs and they are facing the open side of the staging area.

It used to totally frustrate me anytime I would spook a buck out of the area I was going to hunt in the morning. It made me feel as if that morning's hunt was going to be an exercise in futility, and it usually was. Sure, I would have smaller bucks go by, but never the big one. The odds of spooking a mature buck out of an area and having him return later that same morning are as close to zero as you can get. He may return following an estrous doe that pulls him in your direction, but that would be about your only hope of seeing him again that day. As the years passed, I just kept going out earlier and earlier on morning hunts, especially during the rut periods, until it got to the point where I was not spooking bucks with my entry. Arriving at my tree two hours before daylight seemed to be just about the right amount of time for that location. This allowed me to be set up and quiet at least an hour and a half prior to daylight. I never took that big-woods buck, but he certainly taught me a lesson. Several years later, I did take two nice bucks from the same staging area.

How do you set up to hunt a staging area? A staging area setup is exactly the same as a primary scrape setup. In most of the country, the majority of the foliage will be gone by the time these areas are productive. Because these staging areas will receive a lot of deer traffic, you must set up so that other deer will not notice you and ruin your hunt. Hunt a minimum of twenty-five to thirty feet off the ground, so that you are out of the deer's peripheral vision, and try to find a tree with a crotch or other trees behind it for background cover. It is imperative that you do not spook any deer in this zone, and that includes does, fawns, and immature bucks. When hunting a small staging area, set up on the downwind side at a comfortable shooting distance from where you think your potential shot may be. It's a good idea to have two trees set up for different wind directions. In large staging areas, set up in the middle so that as much of the area can be covered as possible during a single hunt. Make sure your stand location is within shooting distance of the best available cover. This will be necessary later in the morning, when a mature buck may come through scent-checking for does that passed through earlier. During midday, the bucks will stay as tight to the best available cover as possible. Make sure your shooting lanes are thoroughly cleared out as well. Your odds of receiving a second opportunity are slim, so you have to be sure you are properly set up and ready the first time.

Do not set up any closer than fifteen yards from a field edge, and never walk the edge of an open cropfield to your stand before daylight or exit along it after dark unless it's a standing cornfield. The cropfield bordered by a staging area will usually be harvested by the time the staging area becomes most productive, allowing a great deal of visibility for the deer feeding in the field. If you spook those deer with your entry or exit, they will change their pattern and stop passing through the staging area during daylight. Once that happens, there is no reason for the bucks to use it during the day either. All buck activity during the prerut and rut phases revolves around doe movements.

Pay close attention while walking to any stand. If you are spooking deer regularly, you are doing something wrong. Choose a different route to your stand if you have to. I would rather walk an extra mile and have a chance at a mature buck than walk fifty convenient yards and spook that buck out of the area.

Never hunt a staging area until it is absolutely ready to hunt. Your plan of attack should be the same as if you were hunting a primary scrape area. Wait until the prerut before you even think about hunting a staging area. Your first attempt should be during an evening hunt. Make sure you arrive very early. If the scrapes are not active or there are not any fresh rubs, do not hunt the staging area. Either turn around and go home, or head for a secondary stand somewhere else on the property. Your extra-early arrival should allow you ample time to get to another spot. Frequent and untimely hunting of such a potential hot spot could be very detrimental to future hunts in the area.

Once you know that a staging area is active, the best time to hunt is in the morning. When hunting in pressured areas, it cannot be stressed enough how important it is to be set up and quiet prior to the dominant buck entering that zone before daylight. In some areas I hunt in Michigan, if I am not in my stand and set up at least two hours before daylight, my chance at a mature buck is ruined for that hunt. With an arrival any later, I either spook the buck out of the area as I walk in or spook him as he approaches the area while I am setting up.

In nonpressured areas, it is not necessary to arrive that early. While I was hunting a large staging area in Iowa in mid-November 2001, the mature bucks would not show up until at least half an hour after daylight. Although I was set up and quiet at least an hour prior to first light, it was not necessary.

Hunting in a staging area that bordered a picked beanfield on a November morning in 1992, I was set up in my tree an hour and a half before first light. Within half an hour, a deer walked straight into the area and bedded down about forty yards from me. It did not mill around and feed on acorns, so I assumed that it was a buck. Just as it was growing light, a single doe entered the woods and started to browse in my direction. The bedded buck stood up and started toward her. When she noticed him, she picked up her pace and passed within six yards of my tree. Within seconds, he was on her trail and presented me with a six-yard shot. This buck was a very respectable eight-point. Although he was not the dominant buck in the area, it was the day before the Michigan gun season, so I decided to take him. This was a prime example of a mature buck taking advantage of the dominant buck's core area while he was elsewhere.

On morning hunts in staging areas, another absolute must is to hunt until at least 2 P.M., all day if possible. As when hunting a primary scrape area, there's always an excellent chance of a mature buck in search of estrous does later in the morning, after all the other deer traffic has passed through. Bucks frequently move into their staging area during midday and early afternoon to wait for the does to pass through later in the afternoon, so get there as early as possible on evening hunts. Midday movements by mature bucks are generally tight to the best available cover, so make sure your stands are set up accordingly.

All this time on stand might seem a bit much, but it's not. When you think about all the time you put into hunting, practicing with your bow, scouting, shopping to upgrade your equipment, watching videos, talking hunting in social groups, setting up trees, and so on, it's not that much of a sacrifice to get up an hour or two earlier during the two or three weeks of the prerut and rut. I'm not saying you should hunt like this every day, but that you should hunt your best spots at absolutely the best times. You should be willing to do what it takes in this short window of opportunity. If you're not getting enough rest, take a morning off and sleep in, or take a nap later in the day. Whatever you do, do it right, and eventually your efforts will be rewarded. It may take a while to be successful, but taking mature bucks in pressured areas with a bow is anything but easy.

CHAPTER 11

Hunting Rubs and Rub Lines

Like all other forms of hunting in pressured areas, hunting rubs and rub lines has to be done very carefully and at the right time in order to be successful. Other than runways, rubs and rub lines are the most visible sign to be found while scouting. There are two nice things about hunting a rub line. The first is that you know the rubs were made by a buck, and the second is that it is a travel route that he is comfortable using. Rub lines are fairly easy to find, indicate a buck's regular travel route, and are easy to set up along and hunt. This sounds simple. It's not! The problem is that rub lines made early in the fall generally connect a bedding area to a feeding area. This means that after a few days of hunting pressure, mature bucks will use their rub lines almost exclusively after dark.

This makes your timing essential. In areas that receive heavy hunting pressure, it's best to hunt rub lines early in the season. Mature bucks still in their summer routine will travel their rub lines from feeding to bedding areas or vice versa. During this time of the season, bucks that are unmolested are more predictable than at any other time of the season. Once their summer routine is interrupted by too much scouting or hunting pressure, mature bucks will still travel along their rub lines, but most of this movement will take place after dark. Most hunting areas remain unmolested from spring on throughout the summer. Often mature bucks, because they have been undisturbed for so long, will bed along the edges of their bedding areas rather than deep within them. This means that your first encounter with your quarry will be without a weapon while scouting. In extremely pressured areas, that first encounter may be your last, and enough to push a mature buck into a nocturnal routine until the rut phases start. This is yet another example of how preseason scouting can be detrimental to success. In nonpressured areas, a mature buck that has not had any life-threatening encounters with hunters will probably

Preseason rubs are proof positive that a buck regularly visits the area.

not pay much attention to a single or maybe several intrusions, but in pressured areas, a mature buck may become nocturnal after his first encounter. Look for new rub lines or check old rub lines just prior to season, during periods of very inclement weather to mask your noise and odor.

In order to take advantage of this early window of opportunity, you should have your tree ready from the previous winter. When I'm hunting a buck that has been around for a few years, I use his rub lines from previous seasons that I discovered while scouting in the winter or early spring. I clear out my hunting locations along those rub lines during the winter, and I hunt these stands at the very beginning of the season. If the buck is still alive, there's a good chance that the old rub line will be worked and I will intercept him. If the old rub line is not worked and there is no sign of him, I will hunt elsewhere. Because rub lines are generally along a buck's normal travel route, they remain fairly constant from year to year, unless there is a change in the property resulting from development, crop rotation, or seasonal loss of a natural primary food source, such as acorns or beechnuts.

Since I'm hunting for mature bucks, I only set up along those rub lines that look like they were made by mature bucks. Rubs made by young bucks are noticeably different. It's important to be able to read rubs

This big buck was found and photographed just prior to season by following his rub line (rubs visible in background).

to get an idea of the size of the buck that made them. Buck rubs can sometimes be misleading, however. You cannot tell exactly what kind of headgear a buck has by looking at either his rubs or his tracks, but rubs will certainly let you know a heck of a lot more than tracks do.

Despite the difficulty of determining exactly how big a buck is by his rubs, there are a few clues that can give you an indication of some antler characteristics. Small bucks tend to pick on small saplings and trees, whereas bigger-racked bucks generally rub on bigger trees and occasionally bushes if available. Most instances where I find rubs on bushes, there are broken branches and a scrape beneath the bush. This is not to say that a mature buck will not rub on a small tree, but if that same buck is using a rub line, you should find rubs on larger trees as well. A young buck usually leaves his mark only on the small stuff. A yearling buck in my home area rarely has more than six points and is very spindly. Rubs made by bucks in this category look as if they were made with the side of a smooth pipe rubbed up and down the tree. There will be few, if any, groove marks on the trees.

Tine punctures in the bark well above the main rub indicate that the buck has tall tines. Tine marks on other trees eight inches to the side of or behind the main rub let you know the buck has either a wide rack or tall

These broken branches and rubs hang over two scrapes (not visible in this photo), a clear indication that the area is being revisited.

tines. Broken branches above the rub indicate a tall-tined buck as well. Young bucks with short tines usually can't get enough leverage to break large branches between their tines. Shredded bark or deep grooves in a rub indicate that a buck's rack has small points around the base or the antlers are heavily pearled. If the rub is on a tree eight inches in diameter or larger, it was most likely made by a big-racked buck. Bushes that are shredded are also usually only from mature bucks.

Individual deer have preferences as to what types of trees they rub, the size of those trees, and how often they rub. Sometimes it's possible to identify a particular buck by his rubs. One buck that I hunted for a couple seasons went out of his way to rub on small cedars, which happened to be a rare tree for the area. In the section where this buck lived, if you found an appropriate-size cedar in some cover along his travel route, it was almost guaranteed to have his rub on it. His rubs always had two narrowly spaced grooves. The one time I saw this buck, the explanation for the grooves became obvious: He had two small points near his brow tines that were about an inch apart at the tips. I hunted this buck for two seasons before he simply disappeared. I think this buck liked to rub cedars because they are relatively soft, and the rubs on these cedars were much more visible than rubs on any other species of trees in the area. There were numerous poplars in the area that usually were torn up, but he

The tine marks on trees beside this rub show that it was made by a buck with a wide, tall rack.

rarely rubbed them. He was absolutely the dominant buck in the section, and his highly visible rubs let everyone know it.

By looking at rubs, you can also determine the best time to hunt a rub line. If all the trees in a rub line are being rubbed on the same side, you can track the rub line to determine whether the rubs were made in the morning or evening, and hunt accordingly. If the rubbed sides are toward the bedding area, then the rub line is being used in the evening as the buck is traveling from bedding to feeding. If the rubbed sides are away from the bedding area, then a buck is making the rubs in the morning while returning to bed down. When you find a rub line while postseason scouting, you should follow it to its destination points, if possible. Quite often a mature buck's rub line will lead you to a primary scrape area or staging area, and it may lead you to one of his exact bedding locations.

On one occasion, I followed a rub line to the neatest little bed I have ever seen. It was an elevated mound covered in moss about four feet in diameter, located in a small cedar swamp. Every small cedar tree near this bed was rubbed. Those rubbed cedars reminded me of no-trespassing signs. The buck had obviously marked his core bedding area with vigor. The moss in the bed was covered with the buck's white belly hairs. This bed looked nearly as comfortable as my bed at home. I never got a chance

The unusual amount of shredding in this rub indicates that the buck's rack was probably heavily pearled near the bases.

to hunt for this buck—the very respectable three-and-a-half-year-old nine-point was hit by a car a week before opening day of archery season.

During what is commonly referred to as the October lull, which in Michigan usually starts around October 5 and usually runs through October 25, I limit my hunting severely so that I do not contaminate my best areas before the upcoming rut periods. Hunting rub lines during this time can be productive, but usually not for the dominant buck in the area. At this time, most mature bucks are normally nocturnal and only use their travel routes and rub lines after dark. Rub lines that you find along open field edges are also made primarily after dark. Mature bucks do not like to expose themselves at any time during daylight, once there has been any intrusion into their core areas. Bucks just do not live to maturity if they make themselves vulnerable in open areas during daylight. This is especially true in heavily hunted regions before the rut.

Once the prerut starts and the mature bucks start to move during daylight, hunting a rub line of a mature buck can produce opportunities if hunted properly. Mornings during the prerut and rut are simply the best time to hunt a rub line. There is a chance of intercepting a buck returning to bed down along his rub line after a night of looking for or chasing estrous does. During the evening, you are simply not as likely to intercept a buck along his rub line in pressured areas. Even during the prerut and rut, mature bucks are still cautious and more nocturnal than other deer. On evening hunts, it's difficult to hunt a rub line close enough to a bedding area to allow a mature buck to pass through before dark without spooking deer inside the bedding area as you approach your tree. This is especially the case if the bedding area is small. The only exception would be on windy, rainy, or wet days. It is much easier to hunt near a bedding area in the morning and sneak out undetected in late morning or early afternoon. When you leave your stand, get down and leave very quietly. Do not walk anywhere you absolutely do not have to. At all times, approach and exit your trees as quietly as you can. During an evening hunt, even if a mature buck hears you approach and enter your tree without spooking, he definitely is not going to get up and exit his bedding area in your direction before dark. Mature bucks in pressured areas are more cautious when moving in the evening than they are in the morning, making it more difficult to get shot opportunities. It's a good idea to stalk the last two to three hundred yards to your tree. Remember, you want to have as little impact on your hunting area as possible.

It is imperative that you be on stand well before first light and as close to the bedding area as possible without risking spooking deer on your way in. After moving all night without human interference, mature bucks seem to move more casually during morning hours. The buck you are after may move through just after first light, but he will probably pass through before it is light and bed down. In some cases, however, during the rut phases, the buck will return later in the morning, after most of the other deer have bedded, to scent-check the perimeter of the bedding zones for estrous does. In doing this, it is possible that a buck will follow his rub line. By this time of the season, there should be an occasional scrape along the rub line as well.

Rub lines are excellent ambush locations, but there are some draw-backs to hunting them in pressured areas during the rut periods. Rub lines are buck travel routes. I prefer to hunt destination points that bucks will seek out and arrive at during midday. Mature bucks often move dur-ing midday to scent-check their primary scrape areas and the perimeters of bedding areas in search of estrous does. Matriarch does know where a dominant buck's primary scrape area is, and they visit these areas when they come close to estrus. Does also leave their scent on licking branches over scrapes to let bucks know of their presence and receptivity. I have witnessed this on many occasions. I do not believe that estrous does will seek out a buck's rub line or follow it. My experience has taught me that rub lines usually connect bedding areas to feeding areas and are along travel routes or field perimeters, which in pressured areas are usually tra-versed after dark by mature bucks beyond the first few days of the sea-son. This is not to say that a buck will not use his rub line at all during daylight, or that a rub line cannot lead to a primary scrape area or staging area; in many cases, it will.

The point is that during the prerut and rut, bucks that move during midday have a certain destination in mind. That destination is rarely a feeding area. In most cases, bucks will be heading toward a primary scrape area or another bedding area. Mature bucks abandon their normal routine of traveling from bedding to feeding, or vice versa, at the exact moment that they become more active during daylight hours. In an attempt to be as effective as possible, bucks often take the shortest route between two points that provides some cover. The search for estrous does is their primary concern at this time. Mature does do not tend to follow the same trails as mature bucks during the early or middle part of the sea-son. In fact, they generally try to keep their distance from the travel corri-dors lined with rubs. Therefore, the buck's rub line or normal travel route is not a focal point for him as the does in the area start coming into estrus.

This leads me to yet another reason why I prefer to hunt destinations rather than rub lines during the rut stages in pressured areas. On most of the properties I hunt, the amount of space I have is limited. A rub line will traverse several properties, with only a fragment actually on the property where I am hunting. If this fragment is not close to a bedding area, it is difficult to pattern a buck's behavior well enough to be able to connect with him on a regular basis. Hunting a destination point is preferable in such situations. If, however, the best sign on your small parcel is a rub line, it is by all means an excellent spot to hunt. Hunting active rub lines during the rut periods can also be justified while waiting for a primary scrape area to reach its peak activity level.

There are other rub formations that are worth looking for. Rub lines or clusters of rubs along the edge of a woods bordering an open field are generally made in the security of darkness. If the field consists of tall weeds or standing corn, however, perimeter rub lines or clusters may be visited during daylight. Whenever there is adequate cover, there is a chance of daylight movement, especially early in the season and during the rut phases. Rub clusters usually also have scrape activity near them.

Another rub location I look for and sometimes hunt is what I call a bedding perimeter rub area. On several occasions, I've found marshes or weed fields that served as bedding areas, with small patches of brush or trees along the perimeter. These patches of brush or trees suitable for rubbing actually attract bucks to enter or exit the bedding area at this point in

Clusters of rubs can be good ambush sites if located in good cover. Bucks revisit them; the question is when.

order to rub their antlers. This is especially true when the remainder of the area has few suitable trees to rub on. A spot like this has numerous rubs concentrated in a small area and provides relatively thick cover just outside the bedding area so that bucks feel comfortable spending a few minutes rubbing before getting on with their routine. When you pinpoint a spot like this, you've discovered an area that specifically attracts bucks. If you set up close to this rub area, but far enough from the bedding area to be able to enter and exit undetected, you have a good chance of killing a mature buck.

Single rubs are interesting sign and can indicate a good buck, but from a hunting standpoint, they are less than spectacular. I would never set up next to a single rub even if it were steaming hot. Although bucks do revisit rubs, the odds of a single rub being revisited that is not part of a rub line, staging area, or near scrapes are extremely low at best.

The significance of rub lines became clear to me in the midseventies. Back then, there wasn't anything in hunting magazines about hunting rubs, and I considered rub lines a sign of a particular buck or bucks using a certain travel route. On a morning hunt on Halloween day in 1977, I set up along a rub line that followed an old, overgrown fencerow. This fencerow connected a large, open wooded area of mature oaks to a rather large swale in the middle of a weed field. From my tree twenty yards from the swale, I could see rubs on almost every sumac and poplar in sight. I had discovered this spot earlier in the season, but even back then I waited until the prerut to hunt what I considered my best spots. Shortly after 9:00 A.M., without having seen any deer, I started to question my stand selection and thought about leaving for the day. In those days, I hunted like everyone else and usually left my stand sometime around 9:30 or 10:00 A.M. On this particular day, because it was an absolutely perfect morning and I didn't have anything else to do, I decided to sit a while longer and just enjoy being in the woods. You can imagine how surprised I was when just after 11:00 A.M., I noticed a very nice nine-point making his way down the fencerow. He was taking his time and rubbing his antlers on just about every other tree. Eventually he stepped into an opening only twelve yards away from me. My shot was good, and the buck collapsed after a sixty-yard sprint. Most important, though, were a couple important lessons I learned that morning. The first lesson strengthened my suspicions that rub lines should not be overlooked, because they indicate a travel route where a buck feels comfortable. The nine-point I shot was a textbook case of a buck using his rub line to return to his bedding area late in the morning. The second, and in my opinion more important, lesson was that bucks like to move during midday during the rut phases in search of estrous does. From that moment on, I began to experiment with staying in my stand for longer periods of time and even started to hunt all day, which was almost unheard of twenty-five years ago.

In heavily hunted areas, there's another reason to hunt rub lines. Since rub lines are preferred buck travel routes and usually offer some cover, mature bucks will use them as escape routes. This facet of buck behavior was reinforced for me on a hunt with Chris in 2000. Chris was set up about twenty yards from an inside corner of a picked cornfield. We knew that a big eight-point had been crossing through that corner to get from a bedding area that consisted of mostly immature pines to a primary scrape area. I was set up about 150 yards from him, along a very distinct and well-used rub line on a ridge that led into another bedding area of tall weeds. Although we were hunting closer together than we normally do, this spot had two separate bedding areas and several feeding areas in different directions, which allowed us to set up close together and in no way disturb each other's hunt.

At 4:30 P.M., the eight-point started making his way toward Chris. The buck was standing slightly quartering toward him at seventeen yards when he took a shot. Unfortunately, he misjudged the angle and hit the buck between the spine and lungs. This is the one shot to the vitals that deer can, and often do, survive. The buck bolted in my direction. At this point, I was a little confused. I could not see Chris or the buck from where I was hunting, but I had heard the shot and saw the buck bound into view. It had been at least fifteen years since the last time Chris missed a deer. The buck gave no indication that he was hit, so my initial thought was that Chris had shot a different buck. The eight-point very cautiously picked his way up the ridge until he got to his rub line. Once he hit his rub line, he turned and began to follow it toward the bedding area and in my direction. Along his rub line, he was walking very determinedly, and I had to bleat to stop his quick pace for a shot. When I bleated, instead of turning to look in my direction, he looked back down the ridge in the direction where Chris was sitting. In doing this, his head and antlers covered his lung area, so I had to shoot a little farther back than normal, but my arrow still found its mark. A couple hours later, I (or should I say we) had my (our) buck. This was a hunt that Chris and I will never forget, and an excellent example of a buck using his rub line as an escape route. In this case, we knew exactly what had happened, and how the buck sought out his rub line as a means of escape. In other instances in areas with hunting pressure, you can sometimes take advantage of a buck using his rub line as an escape route, especially if the rub line is in some form of cover.

CHAPTER 12

Calling and Rattling

Simulating sounds to attract animals for one reason or another has been done for hundreds, perhaps thousands, of years. Whether making the sounds of a small animal to attract a predator, mating sounds during breeding season to attract a mate, or fighting sounds to attract the dominant male, the difficult part is making the right sounds at the right time, when something is within hearing distance that will be interested.

CALLING

Any animal can be fooled with the proper calling techniques if that animal is in the right frame of mind at the time. There is no doubt that if there were a species on earth with a higher intelligence level than ours, they could call us in with the right sounds at the right time. But if we knew we were being pursued, it would become more difficult to get us to respond. Pressured deer react the same way. They are far less likely to respond to calling than deer in exclusive or lightly hunted areas.

When calling pressured whitetails, you have to be a stickler on how often, when, where, and how loud you call. Early in the season, prior to any hunting pressure, deer are much more responsive than after they have been hunted. But mature bucks are generally not interested in responding to calls until the prerut. By this time, around October 25 in the North, most hunters not only have pressured their hunting property, but also have done some calling, making responses from dominant bucks far less likely. In heavily hunted areas, when the time finally arrives in which mature bucks start moving during daylight hours and may be interested in responding to calls, they have experienced enough human activity and faulty calling to easily distinguish it from the real thing.

Calling early in the season can, however, definitely be done successfully if you pick the right times to do it. Subtle sparring, grunting, or doe bleat noises will draw in mature bucks out of curiosity more than anything else during the first few days of season. If you attempt calling in the early season, make sure you are in a location with heavy ground cover. Bucks are simply more comfortable in dense cover and will be more likely to come in close enough for a shot opportunity without the use of a decoy.

Grunting bucks in depends totally on a buck's attitude at the time. I try to do this only when I actually see a buck passing by out of shooting range. If you're trying to stop a buck for a shot, I definitely do not recommend grunt calls designed to use at full draw. Because a grunt is a buck sound, the buck you're trying to stop may well immediately turn toward you to confront the imposing buck, thereby giving you a poor shot angle. Don't just sit in your stand and blow on a grunt call. They don't work that way, particularly if you are after mature bucks. When you grunt, keep the grunts about four seconds apart and very short. Bucks do not make long grunts like you would hear when a sheep bleats. They are very short and punctual.

Doe and fawn bleats can also be used successfully in certain situations. One or two doe bleats can occasionally call in a mature buck during the rut phases, but don't overdo it. Does do not bleat repeatedly like bucks do when grunting, so once or twice is sufficient at any one time. Fawn bleats can work if you see a buck with a doe that will not respond to anything else. If a proper fawn bleat is made and the doe is curious or concerned, she may come in to investigate, and more than likely the buck will follow her in.

Since 1972, when I learned how to make a vocal doe bleat, I have never shot at a moving whitetail. Anytime a buck is moving, whether it be walking or running, I always give a vocal doe bleat to stop him prior to shooting. This must be done while you are at full draw; otherwise, once he stops, he may notice your drawing movements and spook. Knock on wood, this practice has yet to fail me or spook a deer.

RATTLING

On October 1, 1978, just at daylight, I rattled in a buck that had been sparring with another buck out in a hayfield. I was set up in some heavy cover fifty yards from the field in a big pine tree. I could not see the two bucks from my perch. When I could no longer hear them sparring, I did a twenty-second sparring sequence with a split eight-point rack. Within minutes, a curious eight-point was standing broadside at about six yards, presenting me a chip shot that I took advantage of.

Twelve years later, at 7:45 in the morning of October 2, 1990, while hunting in a large bedding area along the edge of a marsh, I heard two bucks start sparring about a hundred yards away. After about five minutes, they quit sparring, so I started gently rolling the sticks in my rattle bag to simulate two other bucks sparring. I made gentle sparring sounds for about thirty seconds, and within minutes, one of the bucks stalked into view. It was a handsome ten-point. He casually walked to within eight yards to give me another chip shot.

Nine years after that, on October 8, 1999, during a morning hunt in a big-woods area, I heard some deer walking through the woods, heading toward a large, marshy bedding area. They were at least a hundred yards away and definitely not coming in my direction, so I decided to simulate a short sparring sequence with my rattle bag. I rolled the sticks in my rattle bag softly for about half a minute. Once finished, I could hear that the deer had turned and started very casually walking in my direction. As they moved closer, I could hear them crunching on acorns. It was an extremely foggy morning, and after a few minutes, two sets of legs appeared under some oaks about forty yards away. By the way they were behaving, I thought they were a doe and fawn. After eating acorns under the oaks for several minutes, they seemed to lose interest in the sparring noises that had originally caused them to come my way. They again changed directions and once more began moving toward the bedding area, which meant they were now walking directly away from me. Since I was way too close to them to do another rattling sequence, especially from thirty feet up in a tree, I pulled my soft inhale grunt call out of my pack, turned away from the deer, and gave one short grunt. Once more the two deer altered their course and started walking straight toward me. I was quite surprised when they finally materialized out of the fog: a very nice mature ten-point followed by an eight-point of the same caliber. Both bucks seemed not to have a care in the world, and when the ten-point was at twelve yards, I shot. In a sudden explosion of survival instinct, the buck dashed fifty yards before he fell headlong into the tall green ferns. Those bucks had been walking so casually through the woods that if I had been aggressively calling, they probably would not have responded. Their response appeared to be purely out of curiosity, nothing more.

Those were three examples of successful rattling early in the season. When you can hear deer casually going about their daily routine without being able to see them, and you are located in an area with some ground cover, you have a good chance of calling them in if your sounds are casual and realistic. Pay attention to the noises the deer are making, and try to replicate them when the time is right.

Rattling can be done with a split whitetail rack, manufactured antlers, rattle devices, or a rattle bag. My tool of choice is a rattle bag with very loose wooden sticks in it. Most commercial rattle bags need to have a stick or two removed, and then be restitched. When you want to get aggressive, the loose sticks can be easily separated in the bag and clashed together louder than in a bag with tight sticks. Mimicking the tickling of the tines or sparring sounds is done by simply rolling the sticks gently or aggressively to get the sound you prefer. Not only is a bag more user-friendly than antlers, it is also compact and does not get in the way when not in use.

After observing many sparring sessions and fights between bucks, it has become obvious to me that bucks spend much more time pushing each other than actually rattling their antlers. The rattling sound during a fight lasts only as long as it takes the bucks to twist and turn their antlers until they securely lock up. Then the push for dominance begins. These fights are very serious, with the loud rattling sequence rarely taking more than twenty seconds. The tine-tickling noises occur during the pushing stages of the battle, until the bucks unlock their horns and start the procedure over again. Therefore, the initial time you spend aggressively rattling should be kept to an absolute maximum of about twenty seconds, with tickling and grinding noises for about a minute thereafter. When bucks spar during the early part of the season to establish dominance, they are much less aggressive. Sparring sounds are much more subtle, and I have watched these sessions intermittently last more than an hour.

While rattling, there should never be constant noises coming from your antlers or bag. There should be at least three times more silent periods than noise periods, and the sequence should not be repeated more than once or twice per hunt in pressured areas. You are not hunting in an enclosure or on extremely exclusive property like most video hunters do, so you should not try to duplicate their aggressive rattling techniques. If a responsive buck is within hearing distance, those first few seconds of aggressive rattling will be enough to get his attention.

When bucks in pressured areas hear loud, aggressive rattling sequences, they are likely to hightail it in the other direction. I have seen this reaction several times. The last time was on a morning hunt in early November 2000 with Chris. We were set up in trees about two hundred yards apart. The plan was that Chris would rattle as soon as it was light enough to shoot. I could see a shooter buck slowly working his way though the funnel of thick brush toward Chris, when he started a rattling sequence that was just a bit too loud and aggressive. The buck instantly took an aggressive posture, listened for a few seconds, then turned and fled the scene in the other direction.

The four times I hunted in Illinois and Iowa, big bucks reacted differently and were quite easy to rattle in. They even seemed to prefer a much more aggressive rattling sequence. The lack of hunting pressure, along with the fact that there is a much higher mature buck-to-doe ratio, made any type of rattling, calling, or decoy use very effective. On some hunts, I rattled as many as eight times and had up to four different bucks respond. That's absolutely unheard of when hunting pressured property.

In regions with tremendous bowhunting pressure, you cannot expect to rattle at any time or place and get a reaction. If rattling is not done properly and at the right time, it will rarely be successful; more than likely, it will be detrimental to your chances of taking a mature buck during that particular hunt. It could also decrease your chances for the remainder of the season. You have to be much more careful not to make mistakes when hunting mature bucks in areas of extreme hunting pressure.

You can rattle at daybreak, just before dark, or in the middle of the day, but midday rattling should be attempted only during the prerut and rut periods. Without question, most of my success rattling in mature bucks has been just at dawn. Whitetails seem calmer early in the morning, probably because they have been feeding and moving all night without fear of contact with humans. Deer that have been bedded all day use more caution when they get up to move in the evening than deer returning to their bedding areas in the morning. This makes it more difficult to get them to respond out of curiosity to rattling. Also, when you rattle in the morning and a buck responds, you are going to see him during shooting hours. The problem with rattling just before dark is that if a response is somewhat delayed, which is often the case in pressured areas, the buck will not arrive at your stand until it's almost dark or after dark. While rattling in the evening, I've had mature bucks wait until it was too dark to shoot before they responded. This creates a situation in which the mature buck is approaching your hunting spot as you are leaving, and usually you will not even be aware of his approach. If you tip the buck off to your presence after rattling, that could be his last response in that location that season, and the last time he comes near your tree. This is why I like to do most of my rattling in the morning.

Bucks have personality differences just as people do. Some bucks are more aggressive than others and are always looking to show their dominance during the rut periods. This is why rattling during midday, from 10:00 A.M. to 2:00 P.M., can be productive. Rattling at this time of day should always take place in relatively thick cover and close to an area where bucks feel secure. You should use a decoy in conjunction with midday rattling to coerce a responding buck to come in close. During midday, bucks will usually hang up out of range without the help of a visual aid. If placed upwind of your stand, a decoy will also help keep mature bucks from circling downwind.

Another key element to successful rattling is location. My favorite place to attempt rattling is along the edge of a standing cornfield, for several reasons. Mature bucks bed in standing corn if the field is large enough and the corn is tall enough. The so-called nocturnal bucks that bed in cornfields are likely to be up and moving at daybreak due to the extreme security that standing corn provides. Mature bucks are more susceptible to rattling or calling if they are up and moving than if they are bedded. On quiet mornings, you can hear a deer moving through a dry cornfield from quite some distance. Thick corn and low light levels at daybreak limit the buck's visibility, which makes him more apt to step out of the corn to see what's going on. During broad daylight, a mature buck is far more likely to hang up three or four rows back in the corn and scan for the deer he thinks he hears.

Sometimes in the morning, after a few minutes, an approaching buck will no longer be certain of exactly where the rattling noises came from. This is especially true if he is cutting through cornrows. If you can hear him coming, tie your rattle bag or antlers to your bow rope, lower it to the ground, and gently jiggle it in the leaves to give the buck direction while he is closing in on you. In such a situation, if you risk rattling again from your stand, you will most likely spook the approaching buck. Rattling sounds coming from twenty-five feet up in a tree are unnatural, whereas the tine-tickling noises coming from the ground are natural. This is especially suited to cornfield rattling, because a deer there can see only a few yards and will move toward the noise coming from ground level. I've pulled this off successfully several times.

In early November 1993, while hunting a narrow finger of sparse woods surrounded by a standing cornfield, I did a short rattling sequence just as daylight was breaking. After about ten minutes, I glanced down to see a large buck quietly passing by my stand through the dew-drenched grass. I had not heard him coming, and by the time I was in position and had my bow drawn, he was past me and behind some brush. There was no way I could get off a shot. I let up on my bow, and he kept moving in the direction of his primary scrape area, which was a mere eighty yards away. He was moving rapidly with his nose to the ground. After waiting about a minute, I rattled for five seconds, then immediately lowered my rattle bag to the ground and jiggled it in the leaves for another ten seconds. The heavy-beamed ten-point turned and marched right back, then circled and approached from the opposite side of my tree. I was in my Ambush Sling, so I was able to slowly move around the tree and into position for a shot. At a distance of twenty-five yards and facing me, he stopped and scrutinized his surroundings for the fighting bucks. Seeming almost a bit irritated that

After this buck passed by my tree without presenting a shot opportunity, I rattled him back to within twenty-five yards.

there were no other bucks around, he turned to cut back to his scrapes. This gave me a quartering-away twenty-five-yard shot, which I made good on.

My next location of preference for rattling is in or along the edge of bedding areas, for many of the same reasons. Mature bucks will be in or near these areas before and after daybreak. They will be comfortable from a night of undisturbed movement and likely to respond just before or after bedding down. When hunting near or in bedding area locations, you need to arrive at your stand even earlier than at the edge of a cornfield, at least one and a half hours before first light, in order to reduce the possibility of spooking any deer returning to bed before dawn. In pressured areas, mature bucks tend to be very nocturnal after a few days of bow season and may head back to bed down an hour or more before dawn. You have to be set up and quiet well before they arrive, or you will spook a mature buck without even knowing it. If the buck you spooked is a mature one, your odds of taking him from that stand, even on a hunt later in the season, are greatly reduced.

One thing to keep in mind is that anytime you set up along a cornfield or bedding area, your odds of seeing deer are very good even without rattling. Try not to ruin your chances by rattling or grunting for an extended period of time. This is a common mistake that saves the lives of many mature bucks in heavily hunted areas. Hunters simply like to rattle and call too much. In pressured areas, less is always best. Along cornfields and bedding areas are where bucks place their rubs and scrapes due to high doe traffic, so even if your early-morning rattling does not get a response, the remainder of your hunt should still be good.

Setting up inside of a bedding area prior to daylight will also work. However, getting out without being detected is nearly impossible and will be costly for future hunts. It will make any mature bucks that become aware of your presence much less likely to respond to rattling in the same area for the rest of the season. This is a method of last resort, sort of like a Hail Mary pass in a football game, and should be saved for the last minute. For example, you might try this on the last day of bow season before gun season starts, if you are hunting a property where a big buck resides and the property gets gun-hunted heavily.

Your first rattling sequence should start as soon as it's legal to shoot, and I mean within the first few seconds. After two or three sequences, put the rattle bag or antlers away for the remainder of the morning hunt. If you see a buck later that is out of range, use your grunt call to try to bring him in before you try rattling again. Individual bucks will frequently grunt as they are moving through an area during prerut or rut, whereas it takes two bucks to spar or fight. If I can see a buck from my stand, there is a good chance he can see the ground below me. This means he may be able to see that there are not any deer where the sound is coming from. In this case, you could be hurting yourself more than helping by rattling. Without the visual certainty of two bucks moving around fighting, the odds of a mature buck coming in close enough for a shot are extremely slim without a decoy. So once you have spotted a buck, you should not rattle unless there is abundant ground cover between you and him to mask his vision. However, one or two short grunts could come from a buck standing behind a little cover. In this situation, a grunt call is much more likely to coerce a buck to within shooting range.

Rattling has proven itself a successful tactic for me from October 1 through late December. Without question, though, I receive the most responses and shot opportunities during the prerut and rut periods. Rattling can work quite well if you do it at the right times and in moderation. Too much of any one thing in the same general area will ruin its effectiveness for future hunts, whether it is rattling, calling, using a decoy, or hunting an area or stand too frequently.

CHAPTER 13

Decoys

The use of decoys has become rather prevalent in the whitetail bowhunting world. Decoys are used for getting bucks in close—bucks that you were not able to get in close without one—and for bringing bucks in from a long distance. They are designed for visual effect and should be placed where they can be seen from the greatest distance. This is why they work well along field edges and open areas. Although I rarely hunt open fields, I often use a decoy when I do.

When using a doe decoy, it should be set up quartering away from you. A buck decoy should be set up broadside to you. Setting up the decoys in this manner should give you a broadside shot at a responsive buck. A buck will almost always approach a doe decoy from the rear and a buck decoy from the front. Never set up your decoy facing your tree or facing directly away from your tree. If it is facing your tree, deer may try to find out what your decoy is so intently looking at and spot you; this is especially true with does. If your decoy is facing directly away from you, your odds of getting a decent shot angle are not as good. Either the approaching buck will be facing you or you will be looking at his rear end.

Always use scent eliminator and rubber or activated carbon gloves while setting up your decoy, and always set up your decoy upwind of your hunting location at a distance of about fifteen to twenty yards. That way, if a deer circles slightly downwind of your decoy, it will still be upwind of you. If it comes directly to the decoy, you'll have only a twenty-yard shot.

When approaching a decoy, a buck will be very focused on it and will rarely take his eyes off it. This allows you time to prepare for the shot. Even though a buck that comes in will be very focused on the decoy, you still want to be set up in a position so that very little movement will be required for a shot near the decoy.

Overuse of a decoy in the same general area will eventually cause the deer to stop paying any attention to it or coming near it. The amount of hunting pressure in the area will also affect the amount of times it can be used before it becomes detrimental to your success. Deer in pressured areas definitely pay much closer attention to anything that could be associated with danger.

There are many decoys on the market. In fact, I have owned seven different styles of decoys since 1992, including two kinds of hard plastic-bodied ones, a blowup, foam rollup, trifold hard plastic, spring-loaded cloth, and a plain cloth decoy that had to be tied off between two trees. These days, though, I use only two types of decoys.

My first choice is the Montana whitetail decoy. It is easily transported in a backpack, only weighs about a pound, is quiet to set up, and looks like a real deer from nearly every angle. It is made of coiled spring steel (similar to that of pop-up blinds) wrapped in cloth, with an actual picture of a mature doe printed on each side. It coils down into a compact, twelve-inch-diameter by two-inch-thick package that will fit into any backpack, leaving plenty of room for your clothing and other accessories. The Montana decoy can be set up so quietly that you don't have to be afraid of spooking deer bedded nearby with the setup procedure like you do with other hard-bodied decoys. Set up the decoy outside in a shaded

Montana decoy (left) and Carrylite decoy.

area to air out for a couple days before you use it hunting. It's also a good idea to purchase a carbon storage bag to store it in so that it does not pick up any foreign odors. A good friend of mine took a big eight-point using a Montana decoy during the 2000 season. He told me the buck's nose was touching the decoy when he shot it. The first season I used mine, a nice ten-point with several broken tines and a couple smaller bucks came in to check it out. They all gave me shot opportunities that I passed on.

My second choice is the Carrylite decoy, which comes with optional antlers so you can use it as a buck or a doe. It's the most realistic-looking hard-bodied decoy, and the included carrying bag can be stored inside the body cavity while in use to prevent deer from detecting its odor. Drawbacks are that it's relatively noisy to set up and very cumbersome to take into the field due to its size and weight. In fact, if you're packing in your stand, bow, backpack, and any hard-bodied decoy, you have your work cut out for you. If you're using it as a buck decoy to hunt for a buck of any size, trim the antlers down to four points so it will not intimidate smaller bucks. The eight-point rack it comes with is fine if you're pursuing only mature bucks three and a half years old and older. I've been using a Carrylite since it first hit the market and have taken a couple good bucks and had many encounters with subordinate bucks while using it.

On an evening hunt in late October 1996, I set up my hard-bodied decoy as a doe twenty yards from my tree on a small knoll in a forty-acre hayfield. An unseasonable snowfall the day before had left a foot of fresh snow on the ground, making the decoy easy to see from nearly anywhere in the rolling field. Two spikes came out into a picked cornfield that adjoined the hayfield and started to feed in my direction. As soon as they caught sight of the decoy, they hurried over to check it out. One of the spikes walked up to the decoy and hit it in the side with his little antlers, nearly knocking it over. The two spikes immediately ran about fifty yards out into the hayfield, stopped, and stared backed at the plastic deer, seeming puzzled by what had just happened, but eventually moved farther into the field to feed.

Soon after the spikes left the field, nine does and fawns stepped into the field from the woods on the other side and curiously started moving toward the decoy. When they got within twenty yards, the matriarch doe halted and started head bobbing and hoof stomping to try to make the fake deer move. After about five minutes of curious attention without a reaction from the decoy, she stomped and snorted a few times and then departed the scene, taking the other deer with her. One of the button bucks in the group had walked up and sniffed the decoy just before mom spooked. Minutes later, a young six-point walked out into the field and also came directly over to inspect the decoy. He hung around the decoy for a few minutes, and then wandered off toward the other nine deer in the field.

When it began to get dark, I pulled out my rattle bag and went through a thirty-second sequence followed by several grunts and a wheeze to try to lure the buck I was after out into the field. Within minutes, the nice eight-point stepped into the field only fifty yards away. He immediately noticed the doe decoy and started to strut toward it. He was only five yards from the fake doe when I released my arrow. It was the first time I had used the decoy in that location, and it was a very eventful evening.

Whenever there is a buck traveling through an area where I cannot hunt from a tree, such as in a weed field, a marsh, or a clear-cut, I try to find the nearest huntable tree where my decoy can be seen from the buck's travel route. Upon sighting the buck, I wait until he moves into a position from which the decoy is visible to him, and then either grunt or bleat, depending on which decoy I'm using, to get his attention. Sometimes you have to get pretty loud to get a buck's attention. During any period of the rut, if the buck is not with a doe, he will generally come right in. A ground blind is advised if there are no adequate trees within easy sight range of the buck's routine travel route. Pop-up blinds are excellent in ground blind situations, but it must be high enough inside that your top bow limb does not hit it when releasing an arrow.

In 1991, I used a decoy to bring into range an eight-point that I could not get close to on two earlier occasions. He was using a runway about eighty yards from any huntable tree, and his rubs along that run made it obvious that it was his primary runway from his bedding to his primary feeding area. When I saw him with his nose to the ground, following a doe that had earlier gone down the same run, I bleated until I got his attention, and he did the rest for me. As soon as he saw the doe decoy, he laid his ears back and started walking toward it, very stiff-legged. The eight-point circled five yards downwind of the decoy, which gave me a fifteen-yard broadside shot. The shot was true, and the buck traveled only fifty yards before expiring within sight of my tree. It felt good to have a plan work so well.

Anytime you are going on a hunt of short duration on property you've never hunted before, a decoy should definitely be in your arsenal. An extremely high percentage of deer that see a decoy for the first time will come within shooting distance. It's almost like having a big deer magnet near your tree, and since you are on a short-term hunt, you do not need to be concerned about overuse.

If you are strictly pursuing mature bucks, you should not use a decoy until the prerut starts, unless you are on a short-term hunt. Big bucks are fairly nocturnal in pressured areas prior to this period, and the use of decoys with any regularity before the prerut will make subordinate bucks and matriarch does shy away from your decoy during the rut stages, when you really need them to respond to it. Once the prerut starts, the use of rattling, calls, and scents in conjunction with your decoy will aid your results, if done properly and in moderation.

Attractant scents on your decoy are not necessary if it is set up at a good vantage point. If you are hunting where there is not much visibility, however, the proper scent for the time of season might lure a buck within sight of the decoy. I've had bottled scents work both for and against me, so I usually just rely on the decoy to do its job, along with some vocal calls or rattling. One scent I do like to use is real buck tarsal gland. During all stages of the rut, I hang a full-rut tarsal gland under the tail of my decoy, whether using it as a buck or doe. I believe that the use of a tarsal gland in conjunction with a doe decoy really arouses a buck's curiosity. Not only does he have a visual to zero in on, but he also has the scent of a potential and unknown rival to pique his interest. The tarsal gland can also be used as a scent drag leading to your decoy setup spot. If you expect mature deer to cut and follow the scent trail, it is imperative that you wear rubber boots and an activated carbon Scent-Lok suit to cover your human odor. It is also a good idea to spray real buck or doe urine on anything you or your clothing comes in contact with, as a precautionary measure to avoid detection.

I almost always set up my decoys as does, even during the rut. If a buck is going to come in to a buck decoy during any of the rut periods, he will also check out a doe decoy for breeding purposes. The only exception to this is if a buck is already with an estrous doe, in which case he may not approach a doe decoy, but he might come in to a buck decoy to show his dominance and run him off.

On a morning hunt in December 1997, I had a big twelve-point pass within thirty-five yards of my doe decoy twice while chasing does. He never paid any attention to my decoy that morning. I think he was so focused on the live does that he never noticed my decoy, which was in plain sight. After pulling the decoy at midday, I took that buck that evening as he was casually heading to a picked cornfield.

If you are hunting a stand where you know you're going to see numerous deer, use the decoy only two or three times during the entire season. Mature does are very curious the first time they see a decoy and generally come within five to twenty yards. They eventually stomp or snort, and then run off. Overuse of a decoy in an area of heavy deer traffic will totally shut down the mature deer's interest and actually cause them to stay a safe distance away from it. This could ruin some of your prime hunting time and potentially spook any buck that may be with the does or nearby. If the buck you're pursuing always has does around him, you should use a decoy only as a last resort.

When hunting open big-woods areas with mature trees, there's usually no set pattern to deer movement. The deer just roam through the woods as they feed on acorns, beechnuts, and other mast. Usually the canopy of foliage from the mature trees keeps the amount of undergrowth to a minimum, allowing a visual aid such as a decoy to be seen from a long distance. Decoys used under these circumstances work extremely well in bringing bucks within shooting range, especially if you limit their use to the right time of season.

A decoy should not be used in a tight, high-traffic funnel unless you are rattling to bring bucks into the funnel and using it for a visual aid. Funnels are used by all deer and should not require a decoy under normal circumstances. Two exceptions to this rule are on short-term hunts or to lure a buck in close enough for a shot in a funnel that is extremely wide.

Rattling and grunting are enhanced greatly by the use of a decoy, because the decoy will appear to the buck to be the source of the sound. Without a decoy, it's likely that a pressured mature buck will hang up out of range. The use of a decoy while bowhunting is not only fun, it is also a serious tactic that can lead to success on hard-to-hunt pressured bucks.

CHAPTER 14

Late-Season Bowhunting

Yes, there are still mature bucks alive after gun season. The question is how to get close to them during the toughest hunting month of the entire season. The weather, lack of foliage, and two hard months of bow- and gun-hunting pressure stack the odds in the bucks' favor. You will be involved in a one-on-one, up-close and personal challenge against a much wiser animal after gun season. But if you're willing to brave the elements, you will enjoy the beauty, serenity, and solitude of late-season bowhunting. This is not a time for the faint of heart. It will truly test your mettle and commitment to this gratifying and magnificent pursuit. Successful or not, once the season is over, you'll know you gave it everything you had.

As the weather is transforming, so are the whitetails. Mature bucks need to replenish their body fat that was lost chasing does during the pre-rut and rut periods. Dominant breeding bucks lose up to 20 percent of their body weight during the three- to four-week period in which their breeding urges totally disrupt their desire to feed. In the northern states, these bucks now must begin feeding heavily if they are to survive a hard winter, and that necessity combined with the second rut are the biggest factors in December and January bowhunting. Many other factors also need to be considered to have a realistic opportunity at taking a mature buck at this time of year. Weather, wind direction, previous hunting pressure, types of terrain you have access to, crops in the area, your ability to dress for the weather, and even the types of trees available to hunt from all play a major role in your chances of success.

The more severe the weather, the greater the necessity for deer to feed. I've sat in trees during snowstorms, cold rain, freezing rain, and ten-below-zero temperatures and watched bucks moving to and from feeding areas. The colder the weather, the more they are forced to feed.

Mature whitetails are most uncomfortable moving in extremely windy conditions. High winds will drive deer to low ground where there is some sort of cover to break the wind. The cold wind penetrates through their fur, causing them to burn body fat much more rapidly in order to stay warm. Only during long periods of high winds will deer be forced to actively feed. High winds also create so much movement of the weeds, branches, corn, or other cover that their senses are not capable of detecting danger as they normally would. Even young deer are very nervous while moving under these conditions at this time of year. Any period of high winds is a great time to do some scouting, because all the movement and noise they cause will mask your own, reducing the probability of spooking any deer. Scouting at this time of year during normal weather conditions is very difficult to do without spooking deer, which would be very detrimental to late-season hunting in previously pressured areas.

Previous hunting pressure has a serious impact on your hunt. The amount of pressure, the number of days that have elapsed without any pressure, and the age of the buck you're after will all have a definite effect on how much daytime movement of deer there will be. It takes very little human presence after gun season to alter the movements of a mature whitetail. Try to find small pockets to hunt that had little or no gun-hunting pressure. Maybe an area that was inaccessible during gun season due to high water is now frozen over, allowing access. Or perhaps you can get permission to hunt some other property now that gun season is over. You must think outside the box and not go back to what you were doing previously.

Is the property you are hunting such that it will hold pressured whitetails after gun season? If there's not a bedding area or food source on or near your property, the realistic odds of success will be near zero. A bedding area for a big buck does not have to be a large area of heavy cover. There needs to be only a small amount of cover for him to feel secure. However, it must be in a location where there has been little or no hunting pressure. The catch is that you must know of these locations beforehand. If you go looking for them and spook the animal you're after, the odds of his coming back to bed there will be slim during the remainder of the season.

If you are tagged out after gun season and you have property on which you know you will be able to hunt for several years, I highly recommend scouting it after gun season for future late-season bowhunting. Keep notes of where you jump deer or where the beds are when there is snow on the ground. Spooking deer at this time will not affect the next season's movements, and it will let you know exactly where they go when pressured. This will definitely help future late-season hunts.

WHERE TO HUNT

In big-woods areas, acorns are the main food source when available. These areas should be set up primarily for evening hunts. Entering these areas prior to daylight for a morning hunt will only spook the deer out of the area and will definitely affect future hunts there. The ideal situation for hunting any food source is to set up in a funnel or well-used travel route leading to it. Never hunt such a stand during an unfavorable wind. It is also extremely important to find routes to your stand sites that allow you to enter or leave without spooking deer. Any noise you make will travel much farther at this time of year, with the lack of foliage and the cold, crisp air.

Cedar swamps are major target areas for big bucks during years with plentiful early snowfall. These are great locations for morning hunts. Bucks are likely to move into these areas after daylight to check for estrous does, feed on cedar boughs, and bed down. In this type of area at this time of year, you need to arrive very early so as not to spook white-tails returning prior to and at the crack of daylight. The deeper the snow, the greater your chances are of taking a buck in the cedars, and the more likely deer are to stay on runways. Very large cedar swamps become deer-yards during winters with heavy snow. Deer feel secure in their yards, and their need for food will cause them to feed during the day, so hunting at any time of day can be productive.

Farmland whitetails concentrate their feeding in cropfields as well as on acorns. If corn or alfalfa is available, this will be their main food source. In most instances, deer feed on acorns before entering picked cropfields after dark. You should have stand locations prepared in these oaks for evening hunts. You can hunt oaks on morning hunts as well, when deer will be feeding in other nearby cropfields at night. Be on stand a minimum of an hour and a half before first light to ensure that you do not spook any mature animals moving out of the crops and into the woodlots before daybreak. Any mature buck still alive at this time of year is going to leave a picked cropfield well before daylight, and you must be set up before he is in transit.

Standing corn is difficult to find this late in the year, but if you do, it should be an excellent place to hunt. If the field is large enough, it's very likely that the dominant buck in the area is living there. This is also a good time to stalk a standing cornfield. Hunting the perimeter of a standing cornfield can also be extremely productive, so long as you are not after the dominant buck in the area. The dominant buck probably beds in the field and moves out only in the security of darkness, which will make him very difficult to kill. Younger, subordinate bucks, which were constantly being run out of the corn by the dominant buck during the prerut and rut periods, will still be moving from their bedding area to the corn to feed.

Picked cornfields and other cropfields are primary feeding locations. Stands at this time should be set up on travel routes at least forty yards from the edge of a field. Setting up right on the edge of a field is setting up for disappointment. There is too great a risk of your being silhouetted on the edge of a field against an open skyline. Deer tend to travel in groups by this time of the season, and if there is a buck in the group, he generally brings up the rear. If you are spotted or winded by a deer passing by, you will probably get snorted at. Sound travels well at this time of year, so other deer will hear this for quite some distance. This could potentially ruin your chances during the rest of that hunt, as well as on future hunts, now that the deer associate danger with your location at the edge of that field. Also, if you hunt a field edge, there is no way of getting to or from your stand without spooking deer. In the morning you spook deer going in, and in the evening you spook them coming out. Deer are a little less cautious when moving through woodlots or cover than they are when they get close to the edge of a field, especially once the fields are picked, so here you are more likely to have the opportunity for a shot as they pass by.

The trees from which you hunt during this period must be large enough to offer some background cover, or else you must get up there a

During winter months, deer travel in groups to make it easier to get through deep snow. Travel routes during the late season are usually used consistently.

Hunting up high is a huge advantage when hunting pressured deer, especially when the foliage is gone. (Here, I'm hanging twenty-eight feet off the ground.)

minimum of twenty-five feet off the ground. If not, your odds of getting away with any movements without being detected are near zero. Pines, cedars, and oaks with leaves are the only types of trees in which you can get away with lower stand heights. Most other trees provide very little cover by this time of year. I have seen videos and television shows where the hunter has his stand only fifteen feet high after all the foliage is down. This indicates that the hunter is hunting nonpressured deer. All deer in pressured areas will notice a hunter hunting that low; even this spring's fawns will spook by this time of the season. In heavily hunted areas, if the large profile of a hunter is so low that he is within the peripheral vision of a deer walking through a barren woods, his chances of getting off a shot are slim.

In early to mid-December, there is a second rut during which unbred does and early-born doe fawns come into estrus. Bucks' energy levels are much lower than they were during the first rut period, and they are far less willing to move during daylight hours, so they do not search as aggressively for does as they did earlier. They will, however, get the job done, with the majority of activity occurring after nightfall. Active scrapes during this period are well worth hunting if they are within or on the edge of cover. Bucks do not waste much energy during this time of year. And they resume a regular movement pattern, which means that any active scrape is likely to be revisited. Any active scrapes now are probably on travel routes between bedding and feeding areas or between two bedding areas. Scrapes between bedding areas should be hunted until at least 2 P.M. for the same reasons as during the prerut. The primary scrape and staging areas that were abandoned by the dominant bucks during the main rut may now become active again if they are close to a current feeding area.

Hunting in a bedding area in which you know a certain buck resides can also be extremely effective; however, this has to be done with care. It must be a morning hunt, and this location requires a very early arrival so that you do not spook deer moving in prior to daylight. You will definitely spook deer when you leave. They may not get up and run, but they will know they have been intruded upon. You simply cannot walk out of the interior of a bedding area at this time of year without making noise. You might get away with a second or third hunt here before daytime movement completely shuts down, but plan on its being one of your last hunts in that area for the season.

AVOIDING DETECTION

Noise is an often overlooked aspect of successful hunting during the late season. The cold weather and lack of foliage to absorb sound make every noise seem as though it is plugged into an amplifier. Clothing made of saddlecloth, nylon, or waterproofed fabrics will make noise when the temperature dips down into the teens. Place your exterior garments outside on a cold night, and check to see how noisy they are when you ruffle them the next morning. This is a good test of how it will sound when you have been sitting in a tree for several hours without moving, and then attempt to draw your bow on a buck.

Your bow also must be quiet on the draw. In cold-weather bowhunts, you may be able to actually hear the arrow drag across the rest. Affix a moleskin pad to the rest on your bow so that no scraping sound is made while drawing an arrow across it. Test your bow by leaving it out in the cold overnight and then drawing it in the morning. Listen for any noises, locate them, and eliminate them.

Practicing with your bow while wearing all your hunting clothes is also important to ensure that you do not slap any of your bulky clothing with your string. Practice from the same elevation as your hunting stands. Make several shots with broadheads to ensure consistent arrow flight.

Opportunities at mature bucks during this time of year in pressured areas are few and far between. You cannot afford to make any mistakes. You must go the extra mile in all aspects of the hunt if you want to be successful.

CLOTHING FOR COLD-WEATHER BOWHUNTING

In northern regions, hunting from late October into January will test not only your skill as a hunter, but also your ability to endure the weather. It is not uncommon to have mornings where the mercury dips down into the single digits. Staying comfortable during this part of the season plays a huge role in your success rate. If you are not properly attired for this type of weather while sitting on stand, you will try to think of excuses to leave when you start to get cold. Being cold or having chills will also magnify any buck fever shakes you may have at critical moments.

Layering is the best way to stay warm. It allows you to walk to your stand without wearing all of your clothing so you do not overheat. Long underwear with wicking properties helps keep moisture from sweat away from your body and should be worn as a bottom layer against the skin. Silk is also a very comfortable and warm material, and although it is extremely thin, it aids as a wind barrier. Wear additional layers, such as a turtleneck, military wool sweater, fleece vest, and/or light insulated garments, over your bottom layer. During extremely cold weather, when you need to wear numerous layers, an insulated vest is an excellent choice as one of the layers. The vest will help keep your body core warm while still allowing arm mobility, which is quite important when you want to take a shot.

Your external clothing or the layer just under it should be windproof or waterproof. A cold wind is without question your worst enemy in the fight to stay warm. If you are sitting on a cold windy day, the wind will eventually penetrate your insulated clothing, no matter how much insulation it has, if one of the outer layers is not windproof or waterproof. Do not put the windproof layer on until you are on stand. These suits prevent airflow, and your undergarments will become damp from perspiration while walking long distances to your hunting location. The moisture is then trapped inside the suit, causing you to become cold much more quickly while on stand.

Several companies produce quiet, waterproof suits that will accept several styles of insulated inner liners for different weather conditions. These suits are excellent for cold weather, because if you are walking long distances, you can pack the exterior waterproof suit and put it on when you get to your stand. During warmer weather, the waterproof shell can be worn alone when hunting in the rain. Quiet, packable, noninsulated rainwear is also available strictly for warm-weather hunting.

In December 1996, I was pursuing a twelve-point that a friend had told me about. To make sure I would not interrupt his possible nocturnal entry into his bedding area, I arrived at my tree two hours before daylight. It was thirty-two degrees and raining as I nestled thirty feet above the ground in my Ambush Sling. I then catnapped, as I sometimes do in my Ambush Sling when on stand early. Upon awakening just before dawn, I could hardly believe what had happened. The rain had turned into freezing rain, and I had at least a quarter inch of ice covering my insulated waterproof suit. As soon as I moved, the ice shattered, sounding similar to the breaking of a window. My bow and arrows were covered in ice and had icicles hanging from them. Needless to say, I carefully exited the ice-covered tree and went home. Despite the weather, I remained toasty warm in that suit due to its insulation and the layers below it, and because it was waterproof, I didn't get wet. I did, by the way, take that buck in December a year later, and it was still a twelve-point.

Wear as little clothing as possible on the way to your stand to keep you from overheating during long walks. Even during cold weather, I often wear just a long-sleeved T-shirt under my activated Scent-Lok suit. My backpack holds all my extra clothing and accessories. I always take more equipment and clothing than I need, regardless of the weather, but if I need something, I've got it. I wear my activated carbon suit to and from my hunting location so that no odor remains on anything my body may come in contact with. Once on stand, I remove my outer clothing and cool down if necessary (it does not take long for the upper body to cool down in cold weather). I then dress in my various layers, replacing my bottom layer, the long-sleeved T-shirt, with my long underwear tops. Now I am cooled off and wearing totally dry clothing. On morning hunts in cold weather, I leave a half hour earlier than normal to allow time to change my clothing while on stand. If you overheat getting to your stand and do not replace the damp bottom layer, you will probably get cold quite rapidly.

An item I have been using for several years is Grabber's adhesive body warmers, 3-by-5-inch air-activated pads with adhesive on one side that were originally designed to treat medical conditions such as arthritis. I stick one over each kidney and one on my chest when I start to get cold. They are designed to adhere to the bottom layer of clothing. These warmers will maintain the perfect temperature to keep you toasty warm. Adhesive body warmers are a fantastic item to use during cold weather, and they will extend your hunting time dramatically. They have made hunting in the cold much more enjoyable than it used to be. Take a quart-size resealable bag with you, and when you remove the warmers, place them in the bag, squeeze the air out, and seal it. This deactivates them so they can be used again later. They last about twelve hours, so you can get two or three uses out of each of them. *Warning:* Do not mistake other air-activated warmers for adhesive body warmers; they are not designed for the same application that close to your body and may cause burns. The other air-activated warmers work fine when used for their specific applications, however, and will also greatly aid in keeping you warm.

On extremely cold days, take along a soft hand muff with an air-activated hand warmer in it to keep your hands warm. The muff should come with a waist strap so that it stays in place during a shot opportunity. The muff allows you to wear lighter gloves, which will give you more feel when you take a shot.

A good portion of heat loss that occurs while hunting is through your head. A Spando-Flage face mask with eye holes cut out, along with a Scent-Lok head cover, keeps my head pretty warm. I will also pack an insulated radar cap if it's going to be extremely cold. Insulated and noninsulated waterproof hats are worth the extra money for their waterproof and windproof qualities.

In cold weather, as in all weather conditions, rubber pack boots are a necessity so that you do not leave any human odor on the ground when walking to and from your stand. The negative aspect of rubber boots is the same as the positive aspect: They do not breathe. This means that your inner boots, any removable insulated liners, and your socks are going to get wet from sweat if you walk very far to your stand. Once your inner boot is damp, it does not take long before your feet get cold.

I took this late season ten-point in a funnel connecting a big woods to a bedding area.

I came up with a simple solution to this problem while hunting in the Shiawassee Federal Goose Refuge about twenty years ago in December. On the first day of my hunt, the temperature with the windchill reached twenty degrees below zero. It was a three-mile walk to where I wanted to hunt. By the time I reached my hunting location, the inside of my boots, liners, and socks were soaking wet with sweat. The wet boots totally changed my game plan for that day. I could not sit for more than two hours at a time before I had to get up and move around to warm up my feet. The next day, I packed dry wool socks in my backpack. I put on a pair of regular white socks, covered them with ordinary plastic bags, and put my boots on over the plastic bags, then walked the three miles to my stand. Once on stand, I changed my socks, placing the sweaty ones in the plastic bags to contain the odor. Now I had dry boots, liners, socks, and feet. My feet stayed warm much longer than the previous day. Whenever I have to walk long distances while hunting, I follow that same routine.

When purchasing boots, keep in mind that their temperature ratings are for walking, not sitting. If you are going to sit on stand for long periods of time during cold weather, buy boots that are rated for much colder temperatures than the temperatures in which you will actually be hunting.

The boot liners need to be dried out after each use, or your feet will get cold much sooner on the next hunt with the already damp liners. An electric boot dryer is very affordable and will dry your boots and liners rapidly.

Wicking socks or wool-blend socks might cost a few dollars more, but they are well worth the money. Socks with a wicking material in them actually pull the moisture away from your feet and into the outer layer of the socks, which aids in keeping your feet warm. Adhesive air-activated toe warmers stuck on your socks over your toes also help in extremely cold weather. If you are going to walk long distances, don't put the toe warmers on until you reach your destination. Otherwise, they will get damp during the walk and won't work as well. Felt insoles will also aid in keeping your feet warm, because they put more air space between your feet and the cold ground.

When hunting in cold, wet weather I sometimes wear my camouflage neoprene waders. They are quiet, totally waterproof, odorless, and very warm. Yes, you will sweat in them, but they are so warm that you will not get cold. They also cover your body all the way up to your chest. Neoprene waders with a quiet waterproof jacket work great in a cold rain.

The late season is a great time to be in the woods. The solitude and cold make this a very challenging time to hunt. If you are prepared for the weather, you will be able to concentrate on the hunt, instead of on just keeping warm.

CHAPTER 15

Recovering Bow-Shot Whitetails

You've done everything right, and the moment of truth has finally arrived: You've shot at and hit that buck you've been after. Now what? Knowing what to do after an arrow has been released is the last, and in many cases most important, step to having a successful hunt. Knowing when to trail a bow-shot deer is just as important as knowing how to trail it. Trailing whitetails shot with a bow and arrow seems to be becoming a lost art. Modern equipment is quite effective, and most deer are recovered within a few minutes when hit properly through the vitals, which is definitely a good thing. However, this has led to a situation where some hunters are no longer proficient at recovering poorly hit deer, simply because of a lack of experience. We as hunters owe these magnificent animals a great deal of respect, and every attempt possible must be made to find any deer that is wounded.

Back in the sixties and seventies, shooting a deer with a bow was a very big deal. A hit deer was in many cases the only shot opportunity a hunter had during the entire season, or perhaps many seasons. Most hunters pursued does as well as bucks, so every deer received the same amount of attention after it was hit. Recurve bows used for hunting usually had only forty-five to fifty-five pound draw weights and produced much slower arrow speeds than modern compounds, making pass-through shots somewhat uncommon. This led to many poor blood trails, requiring a lot of effort and patience to recover the deer.

There are special considerations and difficulties when tracking a wounded deer in pressured areas. When hunting in areas where there are numerous small parcels, pushing a poorly hit deer too soon can easily push that deer off your hunting property onto the property of another hunter who will not allow you to pursue it any farther. Hunting has become so competitive that some so-called hunters will not allow a fellow hunter to recover his wounded animal. I have heard of many instances where the neighboring hunter or property owner will then find the deer and claim it as his own. In heavily hunted states, it happens all the time. And it's not only the occasional neighboring hunter that presents difficulties. In the last ten years, I have encountered more and more landowners who will not allow anyone on their property no matter what the circumstances are. The property bordering one of my hunting locations is owned by very dedicated antihunters who do not allow any access, especially if you are a hunter. These types of situations have actually caused some hunters I know to either give up hunting or hunt only in nonpressured states, where these problems are far less prevalent. While these practices are not shared by most property owners or hunters, they are shared by enough that knowing how to recover your animal in the shortest distance should always be an important consideration.

After a whitetail has been hit, watch it until it is out of sight, and then listen until you can no longer hear it. Immediately mark the last sighting with a landmark that you will easily recognize from the ground. While you're waiting to exit your stand, run the shot procedure through your mind to ensure that you are certain of the angle the deer was facing and where the arrow entered. Knowing the angle and location of entry should give you an idea of what vitals were hit. With this information, you should have an idea of how long to wait before getting out of your tree to begin trailing. Unless the deer expired within sight, you should remain in your stand at least thirty minutes. Do not even get out of your tree to wait on the ground. The noise you make climbing down could possibly spook your buck if he ran just out of sight and bedded down without expiring.

Pass-through shots are common with modern equipment. With most of us hunting from elevated stands, full penetration is without question what we should strive for. A shot with a high entry that does not pass completely through a deer will not leave much of a blood trail, whereas the same shot location with a low exit hole should leave a substantial one.

It is very important when shooting from an elevated stand that you take into consideration the angle of the shot and aim accordingly. How high you sit and how far away your shot is dictate the angle needed for your arrow's entry into the vitals. Do not aim at the same spot on the side of the deer as you would when practicing off the ground. Imagine where the vitals are and adjust your shot entry point accordingly. Practice from a similar elevation just prior to season, and always do some practice shooting with your broadheads to ensure that the arrow flight is the same as with your field tips or resight your bow for the broadheads.

Assuming your arrow passed through the deer, check it and the ground for the following clues to where the deer was hit:

You should practice shooting under conditions as similar as possible to actual hunting conditions, including height off the ground.

1. Blood with small air bubbles in it indicates a lung hit.
2. An abundance of thick, coagulated blood usually means that a main artery (jugular, femoral, liver, heart) was hit.
3. A good blood trail but not a tremendous amount of blood could indicate a meat hit or small artery hit. Without an obvious pass-through, this could mean just about anything.
4. Gritty green or brown substance mixed with small amounts of blood indicates that your arrow passed through the stomach or intestines.
5. A mixture of stomach matter along with quite a lot of blood indicates a hit toward the back of the rib cage, which probably caught both stomach and liver. This shot should leave one or two blades on your broadhead duller than the rest from hitting a rib. This could also mean a stomach, liver, and lung hit if the deer was quartering toward or away from you when you shot.
6. Roughed-up or dull blades indicate that bones were hit. This is important to note with a questionable stomach and liver hit.
7. Tallow on the shaft more than likely means a high hit along the tenderloin, a brisket hit, or a high hindquarter shot. Though tallow is generally not a good sign after a direct broadside shot, it

does not mean much with a severely quartering shot or a shot from a high angle.

Taken alone, hair on the ground is not the best indicator of where a deer was hit. You have to look for other clues for an idea of what type of hit it was. Deer vary in color from reddish brown to dark brown. Only when I see white hair on the ground do I pay any attention to hair. White hair on the ground indicates either a low exit hole from a shot that was straight down or had a very low entry, or a severely quartering-away hit from an elevated stand. White hair can mean a single-lung hit, a gut-liver shot, or any other hit where the arrow exits low through the white belly hair. It can also mean a shot that just grazed a deer's belly or brisket. Look at pictures in magazines or check out a roadkill, paying close attention to where these white patches of hair are located. This will give you some indication of where your arrow hit if you find white hair at a shot site.

Each type of hit mentioned above has to be handled in a unique way.

1. The ideal shot is a double-lung shot. There should be good blood at, or very near, the point of impact with a pass-through shot, and even without a pass-through, there should be ample blood for a quick recovery. This animal will rarely make it farther than a hundred yards and should be very easy to trail. In many instances, lung-shot deer have expired within sight of my stand. In the last seven years, since using inch-and-a-half cut mechanical broadheads, I've watched 70 percent of the bucks I've taken expire. In dry conditions, you will often hear a crash within a few seconds after the hit. The location of that crash is where you should find your expired deer.

   A straight down or severely angled shot in which you are aiming at the lungs will probably enable you to hit only one lung. In this case, the deer should be allowed more time to expire. The blood has to fill the shot lung and then flow over into the good lung before there is any chance of the deer dying. Deer can live with one good lung, just as humans can, and unless your arrow passes through an area of lung where there are large arteries, they often will survive. I've taken three bucks that had previously been shot through the outer edge of one lung without killing them. I suggest aiming a bit farther back, into the liver area, whenever a severe angle is presented. My confidence in recovery is much greater with a liver-hit deer than with a poor single-lung-hit deer.

The center of the lungs should always be your target area with a good broadside or slightly quartering-away shot. Lungs present a much larger target area than any other vitals, thus leaving some margin for error. The heart is a very small target that is partially protected by the shoulder blade and leg bones. Even though Dart systems and 3-D targets give you more points for heart shots, aim for the lungs on the real thing. If you hit the heart, you almost missed. A double-lung-shot deer also will expire faster than a heart-shot deer. A lung-shot deer actually drowns from the blood filling its lungs, which does not take much time. A heart-shot animal runs until it pumps all the blood out of its system, which in many instances will take the animal twice as long to expire. In most cases, a double-lung- or heart-shot deer will run full throttle until it expires. A heart-shot deer that takes longer to bleed out will go farther before expiring, possibly making recovery more difficult.

2. If a main artery was hit, you should have a great deal of blood from shot site to expiration site. A high entry without an exit hole with a heart shot would be the only exception. The obvious reason is that the chest or body cavity will contain most of the blood internally. On any of the hits covered so far (other than a single lung), your deer should be easily recovered. You do this by following the blood trail or starting where the deer was last seen or heard, and making circles that progressively get larger.

3. A flesh wound or meat hit more than likely will not kill a deer. However, any time you hit an animal, you must make every effort possible to recover it or discover whether or not you killed it. Blood trails can be very misleading at times, and when you put a broadhead into a meaty part of a deer, it is going to bleed. If nothing plugs the hole, you will have a sufficient trail to follow for a while. In December 1967, I hit a doe just above its left rear hoof. There was snow on the ground, and the blood left in her hoofprint enabled me to track her. After about a mile and a half, I was able to get close enough to finish her off with a chest shot. I hit a small but main artery in the leg. I could not possibly have trailed that deer without the presence of snow.

With ample snow, you should follow meat-hit deer as soon as possible. If a good artery was hit, your chances of recovery are decent, because you are keeping the deer's blood pressure high by pushing it, which will cause it to continue bleeding. If you did not hit an artery, the blood trail will eventually diminish and end. If there is not any snow, give the animal about four hours before trailing. This will allow the deer time to bleed out if a main artery was hit, or allow it to bed down (lowering its blood pressure) and let the blood coagulate in the wound, which will cause the bleeding to stop. If this deer is not dead, you may jump it when you begin tracking. If this happens, you should leave the deer alone for another four hours before starting another attempt at recovery. Trying to follow this deer right away will most likely drive it into a remote area, where you probably would not find it even if you hit a main artery, resulting in a wasted animal. A deer with a flesh wound will eventually just stop bleeding and usually live to be hunted another day.

4. Way too many animals are lost to the dreaded gut shot. The procedure for this shot is simple. If you know you made a gut or intestine shot, quietly get out of your tree and get out of the area, go to dinner, read a book, or go home and fix that leaky faucet. This deer must be given plenty of time to expire. Do not even walk in the direction the deer went for at least four to eight hours, depending on the weather. If it's cold enough that the animal will not spoil, give it even longer. Nine times out of ten, a gut-shot deer will travel no farther than two hundred yards before getting sick and bedding down. If you leave it alone long enough, it will probably be dead when you return. I've given gut-shot deer in December as long as sixteen hours before attempting recovery. Generally speaking, the larger the animal, the longer it will take to expire. This is true of any type of hit. The drawback to this shot is that there will be very little blood, if any. The deer will also head for the nearest, heaviest cover.

Knowing your hunting area is very helpful in this situation, because a lot of searching could possibly be required, especially early in the season when the foliage is still heavy. So get as many friends as possible to help look, and take your bow with you just in case it's not dead. Unlike a deer that dies in midstride and falls to the ground all sprawled out with its white belly showing, this one will probably be bedded nice and neatly in a hard-to-find place. Check in creeks, ponds, or any water in the area. Poorly hit deer seem to find comfort in cold water; it must be soothing to their wounds. I've recovered several bucks that died in water.

If you are expecting rain, still wait the same amount of time. If this animal is pushed, your odds of recovery will be greatly reduced, and you will probably end up in the thickest, nastiest swamp or brush in your hunting area. If you know it's going to snow or it is snowing and you are expecting a lot of it, then you have no alternative other than to push the deer. You will be following fresh tracks and should eventually get another opportunity to finish him off.

5. The combination stomach-liver hit is also very common. The reason gut-shot and liver-shot deer are so common is that in their excitement, many hunters tend to body-shoot rather than pick a spot. The result of this excitement is a gut shot, liver shot, or both. Anytime you cut the liver, it is a fatal shot. The liver is between the lungs and the stomach and extends to the last rib. This is why you know that if there is a dull blade on your broadhead after you body-shoot a deer, there's an excellent chance that the liver was hit. Liver-shot deer show great variation in the length of time it takes for them to die. I've had liver-shot deer expire in ten minutes and others still be alive the next day. The reason for this is that if you do not cut one of the main arteries in the liver, it will take a long time for the animal to bleed out.

   A liver-hit deer will get sick very quickly and not travel very far before bedding down, usually not much more than a hundred yards. This deer should be left alone for at least four hours. Unlike a gut shot, a liver hit will leave a substantial blood trail for some distance. If you push a liver-shot deer in which a large artery was not hit, the blood trail will eventually stop. This will make recovery very difficult. If you jump a deer shot in the body cavity at any time while trailing him, stop, mark the spot, and give him a few more hours to expire before resuming your search.

6. A solid bone hit such as a shoulder or knuckle without any penetration will not kill a deer. You should make every effort possible to recover your arrow and do enough tracking and sign reading to make certain that you did not penetrate into any vitals. If you discover any sign that you may have mortally wounded a deer, it's your responsibility to do everything possible to recover it.

7. Finding an arrow shaft coated with tallow is not a promising sign. However, with a rear, frontal, or high entry (from a tree stand only), your arrow can have tallow and still have passed through the vitals. When your arrow exits through tallow, the tallow will somewhat plug up the wound, so do not expect to find a lot of blood. The tallow will also clean off your arrow, not leaving much sign as to what might have been hit internally. This hit should be treated similarly to a gut shot unless you are sure that the arrow passed through some other vitals.

Whenever you are trailing a deer, try to keep at least two markers (anything from sticks stuck in the ground to people helping you track the deer) ten feet apart on the trail to give a direction to go by. Also note the direction of any blood splatters on the leaves, in order to pick up on tempo as well as any sudden turns the deer might have made. If the blood starts getting sparse, slow down, look closer to the ground, and check where you put your feet prior to taking each step. On many occasions, I've had to go over the same trail several times before spotting specks of blood. Also look on trees, under ferns, and on branches. Often with a body hit that is not bleeding very much, you can find more blood off the ground than on it from the deer's body rubbing against brush or weeds. In many instances with a bad blood trail, you can actually go faster by looking for kicked-up leaves or dirt, especially if it has rained recently. This makes any alterations on the ground very easy to identify.

Deer will almost always take the easiest route to get to their destination when they are wounded. When you are trailing a deer that's not leaving much blood, check runways, lanes, low spots in fencerows, and holes or openings in fences to try to pick up the trail again. If you are finding consistent drops of blood through a wooded area and the deer enters a grass or weed field, in which it is difficult to trail, mark the last two blood locations. Move straight across the field and start looking for blood just inside the woods, where it will be much easier to find on the leaves. If you think the deer expired in an area of tall weeds, marsh grass, or tall ferns, climbing a tree will enable you to look down into the tall stuff for a carcass or white belly if a blood trail no longer exists.

If you have lost the blood trail, there is a product that can help, called Starlight Bloodhound. When sprayed after dark (it only works after dark), it glows bright blue on even a speck of blood not visible to the naked eye. It actually works best after a blood trail has been totally washed away by rain. It glows when it contacts the hemoglobin found in blood. Even though the rain may have washed the color away, the hemoglobin still exists and is diluted with the rainwater into a much larger area. I used this product for the first time on a two-day-old blood trail that had been totally washed away by rain. There was no visible sign of blood whatsoever. When I sprayed the area where the last blood was found prior to the rain, the results amazed me. It was like following the yellow brick road. This product will not replace good, old-fashioned tracking when you have a visible blood trail, but it can definitely help in certain circumstances when blood is extremely difficult to find.

If you hit a deer that runs into a large cornfield, there is a good chance it will run down a single row. In this case, get a friend and have him cut over twenty rows, counting the rows as he goes. Tell him to then walk down that row in the same direction that the deer is traveling about two hundred yards. Once he covers that distance, he is to cut back the twenty rows, putting him in the same row that the deer is in. Have him set up a simple ambush site one or two rows off to the side. Give him twenty minutes or so, and then continue trailing the deer. The odds are very good that he will get a shot as you push the deer past him. It's much easier for a wounded deer, be it a buck or doe, to travel between rows than to cut through them. This same setup can be used if you are pushing a deer toward a known funnel.

Any time there is any question whether to immediately search for a deer or wait to begin your search, I recommend that you wait. Your odds of recovery will be much greater if you allow a deer time to expire. Being patient is just as important in the process of recovering a wounded deer as it is in getting the shot in the first place. Recovering poorly hit whitetails is definitely an art form. It may not be fun, but it must be done from time to time and is an important aspect of bowhunting.

CHAPTER 16

Fitness and Nutrition

Hunting pressured bucks can be strenuous. Physical preparation for a season of little sleep, long walks, and even longer hours spent on stand is one of the most important yet overlooked aspects of the hunt. An exercise program can be instrumental to success, in that it prepares the body as well as the mind for the occasionally grueling challenges faced while hunting. No matter where you hunt, preparation is often the most important component of successful bowhunting for mature pressured bucks, and your body is the only thing over which you have nearly total control. By doing some basic weight lifting, cardiovascular training, and stretching, you can help your body to prepare for up to three months of climbing trees, walking in full gear, missing meals, and, hopefully, dragging that buck out of the woods.

The weight training element of my fitness program is actually a strength maintenance program. I am not doing any power lifting. Too much muscle can actually be detrimental to hunting pressured deer, because it is nonflexible bulk. Three days a week I work my upper body by doing bench presses, military presses, curls, triceps exercises, and pull-downs, all of which can be done using a set of dumbbells. My workout consists of three sets of fifteen to twenty repetitions for each exercise. I also work my stomach with sit-ups and crunches. There is a considerable degree of adaptability in this exercise program, which means that I can vary the workout according to how I feel and how much time I have outside of my work schedule. Your priority when designing an exercise plan should be to get to a level of strength that allows you to feel generally healthy and to be confident when climbing trees.

Supplementing weight training with cardiovascular exercise will get your entire body fit, allowing you to cope more easily with the stresses of bow season. My cardiovascular workout is relatively simple: I jog or ride a stationary bike for twenty to thirty minutes three or four days a week. I usually do this indoors on a treadmill or a home trainer, but when the weather allows I also enjoy getting outside for a run or a bike ride. When beginning a cardiovascular workout, do not overexert yourself, especially if you are not already fit. If you start slowly, you can build cardiovascular fitness through steady progression, but trying to go too far beyond your capabilities could result in serious injury; better to be initially slow and cautious than fast and furious with damaging results. If you are over-weight, smoke, or have any other health problems, consult your doctor before attempting any fitness program. Whether you jog, ride a bike, or walk, the important thing is to get out there and get fit. This makes bowhunting easier and much more enjoyable.

Stretching is an integral part of a bowhunting workout program, both to increase flexibility and to prevent exercise-related injury. Spend a few minutes before each workout with light stretching, which helps to keep your body flexible and your movements smooth and fluid. Flexibility can be easily lost without continual maintenance, but, with just a few minutes of stretching before and after each workout, you can maintain and actu-ally increase your flexibility. Flexibility is particularly important when you need to climb in and out of stands as easily and soundlessly as possi-ble. When I'm encumbered with several layers of clothing on cold morn-ings, those steps can seem a long way apart, but the flexibility I have gained through stretching makes climbing easier.

Regular practice with your bow completes this program. In addition to developing your confidence and concentration, you are training your muscles for the demands of shooting. If you cannot practice with your bow, I recommend using a bow pull, an inexpensive device that simulates drawing and holding a bow. Pay attention to your form while doing this exercise, so that you don't train yourself into bad habits. Practicing with a bow pull will help to keep you from shaking while holding at full draw for a shot, and can be slipped into almost any free moment of your day.

I begin my exercise program in January after I've given myself a cou-ple weeks to recover from the recent strains of the season, and continue through the year until just prior to season, when I begin the final prepara-tion of my stand locations. Last-minute scouting, in-season scouting, and hunting itself will provide more than enough exercise for the next few months, and continuing to exercise during season will wear your body down quickly. If you are serious about pursuing mature pressured white-tails, the work you'll put into successful hunting will render any addi-tional exercise counterproductive.

During season, it is imperative to eat right and to get as much sleep as possible, so you can maintain your strength through the strains of the season. Getting enough sleep during bow season is admittedly difficult: By the time you get out of the woods, eat, get to bed, and wake up early the next morning, the amount of sleep you get is just not enough. If you hunt a few days in a row, you will probably find yourself suffering from major sleep deprivation. You can do a couple different things to counter lack of sleep. Hunting tactically—hunting your best stands only when they are absolutely ready to be hunted—means that sometimes, especially during the October lull when timing and conditions are not always right, you may not hunt for several days. On days that you are not in the woods, you should get as much rest as possible, so that you are prepared to go out when necessary. Another way to get a refresher, especially during the rut phases, is to sleep in occasionally and arrive at your stand around 9:00 A.M.; on a day like this, you should remain on stand until at least 2 P.M., or even until dark. Midday hunting during this time can be very good if you find the right location, and the extra few hours of sleep will help your mental awareness.

Although eating well becomes almost impossible while spending long periods of time on stand, trying to eat a balanced diet during bow season is important. I carry some soft granola bars and fruit to my stand to offset some of the pitfalls of poor nutrition. During the prerut and rut periods when hunting really starts to get interesting, it is possible to suffer from almost total loss of appetite, at which point you should use a couple of diet supplements and take a good multivitamin. This way you can be certain that your body is getting at least some of the vitamins and nutrients that it needs. This also helps keep me going and I believe makes me more resistant to illness. Between hunts and on days off, make it a point to eat vegetables, fruit, and grains. These foods will provide you with the necessary, extended energy and endurance. I know that if I do not eat that my hunting will suffer, so I make a serious effort to eat well when I get the chance.

There are also diet elements that you should avoid during bow season, with stimulants like caffeine topping the list. Like most people, I enjoy a good cup of coffee in the morning, but coffee is the first thing that I cut out of my diet because it's simply more trouble than benefit when hunting mature bucks. Although caffeine raises your pulse and wakes you up, it seems to quickly let you down even lower than where you started. Even the initial benefits of a stimulant can have hidden repercussions, like heavy sweating while walking long distances in the woods. Hunting requires long periods of concentration and alertness, which are maintained in part by avoiding sudden rushes of mental or physical energy. Beverages containing caffeine are also diuretics that stimulate the kidneys and bladder, leading to frequent urination, and I just do not like leaving any scent in the woods. Opinions vary widely regarding the effect of human urine on deer behavior, and some even claim it attracts deer. However, seeing as deer scent-mark their scrapes with urine, they must have some sensitivity to its smell, and human urine definitely does not smell like deer urine. Given all the uncertainty on the subject, you should try to play it as safe as possible and not leave any scent in the woods, including not peeing anywhere near where you hunt.

Since scent control is so vitally important, it is advisable to avoid spicy food during hunting season. I especially try not to eat anything that contains onions or garlic. If you've ever encountered someone even a day after they've eaten this type of food, you know how it affects their body odor. Just imagine how this smells to deer.

All the exercising you did prior to the season will definitely help your body cope with stress. However, you should also take a morning or evening off occasionally (depending on which period is best in your hunting area), to give yourself time for needed rest. This will in turn help you to be more alert when you return to your stand. By staying in shape and eating right, you will be able to increase not only your enjoyment of hunting, but also the mental energy that will maximize your productivity in the woods. Being fit will make hunting much less tiring, which should help your success.

CHAPTER 17

Equipment

The name of the game in hunting pressured mature whitetail bucks is preparation. Being prepared means having the right equipment to be able to respond to anything that might happen. You cannot accomplish this by just stuffing your pockets with a few things. You must have all of the right equipment all of the time. And this equipment must be checked frequently to make sure it will work as designed when needed. Attention to detail is very important. Following is a list of things I carry into the woods when I bowhunt, both the basics and other gear that I feel is necessary for most events that may occur in the field.

THE BASICS

Bow. Your bow must be set up for hunting, not target shooting. Check your entire bow for any noise, especially during the drawing process. Drawing and shooting must be made as silent as possible. Things to check for noise are limb pockets, wheels, cables, cable slide, and loose parts on attached accessories. It is essential to use string silencers and limb dampeners, and to cover your arrow rest with felt or other soft material so your arrow does not make any noise when drawn. I've watched several videos in which I could hear the arrow drag across the rest as the hunter was drawing on a huge buck. I guarantee those videos were made in a controlled environment, because the hunter would never get away with that when targeting a pressured mature buck. Other than being able to hit what you shoot at, the most important element to the actual shot at an animal is a bow that is silent on the draw. This is much more important than any noise a bow makes after the arrow is released.

Sights. Always use easily adjustable sights with pins that are visible in low-light conditions. Use a strong pin guard so that your pins will not get bumped or bent. My preference is a sight in which the windage (right and left) and elevation of all pins can be adjusted at the same time as well as individually.

Peep sight. If you must use a peep sight, make sure the hole is large enough to see through in low-light conditions. I have heard many stories of hunters who drew on big bucks in dim light and were not able to get off a shot because they could not see their pins through their peep sights. For target shooting, where a tiny margin of error can make a difference, they are definitely useful, but I find them unnecessary for hunting. The vital area on a deer is quite large, and an inch right or left does not make much difference, so within the normal twenty-five yard range of most shots, peep sights should not be necessary.

Kisser button. The use of a kisser button is necessary for many hunters. It is similar in application to the rear sight on a gun, giving you a consistent rear anchor point. By attaching a kisser button to the bowstring, and drawing it to the corner of the mouth before shooting, many hunters can reduce accuracy problems associated with a floating anchor point. I don't use one, but I've seen dramatic improvements in the accuracy of friends who do.

Arrows. If you hunt with aluminum arrows, don't use your practice arrows for hunting. Aluminum arrows tend to get tiny bends and dents in them when they hit each other and are pulled out of targets during practice sessions. These often unnoticeable flaws will affect your accuracy. It's a good idea to have a set of practice arrows and an identical set of hunting arrows. Carbon arrows (without aluminum cores) remain straight unless they are broken, so practice carbon arrows can also be used for hunting without fear of poor flight, so long as the fletching is in good shape.

Detachable quiver. Use a hooded quiver that holds your arrows securely and quietly yet still enables you to get arrows in and out easily during cold weather. I also recommend using a detachable quiver, along with a quiver adapter that will screw into a tree to hold your quiver while hunting.

Broadheads. Use a head with a cut diameter that's appropriate for the poundage you're shooting. Make sure your broadheads fly true out of your bow before hunting with them. Never assume they will fly the same as your field tips.

GEAR
Activated Scent-Lok odor-adsorbing suit. Activated carbon suits should be considered your best bowhunting tool aside from your bow and arrows. An activated carbon suit allows you to go undetected by deer that come in or pass by downwind and is an absolute necessity for

consistently getting close to pressured mature bucks. I would not even consider hunting without one. (See chapter 5.)

Ambush Sling. The Ambush Sling is a great tool if you want to have the most mobility possible for those times when you need an instant change in locations. (See chapter 4.)

Fanny pack or backpack. In order to be prepared for anything that may happen while in the woods, you have to have the right equipment. That equipment must be transported, and a good pack is essential. It should be made of a quiet material, such as fleece or micro fabric, that is washable or lined with activated carbon, and it should have several pockets so that you can keep your items separated. My preference is a backpack with a main pocket of at least 800 cubic inches for carrying extra clothing (keep in mind that I live in Michigan).

I also keep in my vehicle a freelance fanny pack with twenty tree steps, reflective tacks, saw, gloves, and a climbing harness. This pack is used when I want to freelance into a new area or hunt a different tree. It contains everything I need to quickly set up a new tree. I wear it below my backpack only when I think it may be needed.

Every time I go hunting, I consistently use the same pockets for the same items. This allows me to get out whatever I need without having to

Backpack and standard equipment: the Ambush Sling is sitting rolled up at the bottom left corner of the backpack.

look in the pack. When you need something out of the pack, knowing exactly where everything is saves time and, more importantly, avoids excessive movement.

Rubber boots. These are another absolute necessity to keep your odor off the ground while walking to and from your stand. Air out new rubber boots until they lose that new rubber odor prior to use. (See chapter 5.)

Rope. It is a good idea to hunt from at least twenty feet high or higher, especially once the foliage is down. My recommendation is to carry a quarter inch-diameter rope at least thirty feet in length. The larger-diameter rope will not get tangled and knotted up like heavy string will.

Bow hangers. Carry several of these for hanging items like your rattle bag, pack, bow, and so on.

Quiver holder. Use a screw-in quiver adapter to attach your quiver solidly to a tree. I always remove my quiver from my bow when hunting. If you leave your quiver attached to the bow, it's one more item that can potentially make noise on the shot, and it also limits your range of shot mobility. With brightly fletched or crested arrows, it's also possible that a deer might notice you preparing for a shot if the quiver is left on the bow.

Flashlights. Always carry a couple of flashlights. I use a small penlight flashlight while climbing trees and a larger flashlight for blood trailing or navigating through the woods in the dark.

Rattle bag. Carry a rattle bag or a set of rattling antlers. (See chapter 12.)

Grunt calls. I always carry two grunt calls with me: an inhale call and an exhale call. The exhale call is louder. Use whichever call is appropriate for the situation. (See chapter 12.)

Reflective tacks. These should already be in place prior to hunting, but I carry some with me anyway and frequently find uses for them. I've used tacks to mark a blood trail I will return to after dark and to mark recovered kills I plan to retrieve later with help. When the foliage is on the trees, it's amazing how difficult it can sometimes be to return after dark and find your deer again; the reflective tacks will make the task easier. (See chapter 3.)

Binoculars. It's a good idea to carry compact binoculars with a good field of vision in low-light conditions. I suggest using a set of at least 8× magnification with a thirty millimeter lens. You never know when you might discover a buck's travel route in the distance.

Tree steps. I always pull the bottom six tree steps and carry them in my pack. The tree steps remaining in the tree will be above eye level if another hunter happens to be scouting the area. (See chapter 3.)

Bow holder loop. This attaches to your belt and allows you to hold your bow in a ready position without supporting the weight with your arm. I use this only when a potential shot opportunity is unfolding; otherwise my bow always hangs on a bow hanger.

Face mask. I prefer a Spando-Flage mask with the eyeholes cut out. It stays tight to my face and does not affect my anchor point or release. It also helps keep my face warm during cold weather.

Rangefinder. A laser rangefinder will come in handy on shots over twenty yards. Anything under that distance should be shot with a single close-range pin. I take a rangefinder only when hunting in open areas where a longer shot may be possible.

Antihistamine tablets and cough drops or syrup. Usually by the time the prerut rolls around, so do cooler temperatures, and you may find yourself with a cold or cough. Such illnesses cause extra noise and movement. If necessary, take along antihistamines, cough drops, and a bottle of cough syrup and use as needed, keeping them in a sealable plastic bag if they have an odor.

OTHER ITEMS

Air-activated hand and adhesive body warmers
Water bottle
Pee bottle
Compass
Knife
Sierra tooth saw
Scent elimination spray
Safety belt (for tree-stand users)
Tarsal gland, scents
Sealable one gallon plastic bag (for storing sweaty clothing)
Extra clothes
Extra batteries
Extra bulb for flashlight
Toilet paper in a plastic bag
Carbon gloves for climbing trees
Arm guard
Large safety pins (for securing any loose clothing)
Extra tab or release

CHAPTER 18

Some Final Words

Hunting for mature bucks in pressured areas is difficult and requires hard work, discipline, dedication, patience, and time. There just are not any shortcuts to consistent success. The harder and more precisely you work, the more effective you will become. And like everything in life, hunting for pressured mature bucks is a learning experience. Success will not happen overnight. I started bowhunting in the midsixties and did not kill a two-and-a-half-year-old buck with archery equipment until the early seventies. It took me nearly a decade of trial and error before I could connect on a buck that was not a yearling. In those days, I made every mistake in the book. None of the adult men in my family hunted, so I had to teach myself. Although this was a handicap, I was free to make mistakes without being inhibited by a traditional hunting group's bad habits. This meant that I was forced to learn how to bowhunt by responding to deer behavior, and I had to figure out this behavior on my own. I credit the deer that busted me in the early days with teaching me how to hunt. I did pick up a few tips from various mentors through the years, but usually I hunted alone or with a few friends who were nearly all in the same type of situation. Through it all, I kept refining my hunting techniques and eventually started to improve.

When you bowhunt for pressured mature bucks, you cannot afford to become complacent, or you will never get any better. Always question whether you are making mistakes, and try to learn something every time you make one. This attitude is a big step in the process of becoming proficient at killing mature bucks.

I have messed up on more nice bucks than I care to admit. Those unsuccessful attempts have been some of the most important and pivotal hunting experiences in my life. Every time I missed or messed up on a big buck, I learned a lesson, and these lessons formed the foundation for my hunting technique. Not only did these bucks teach me how to hunt better, they also taught me humility. Every time I thought I knew what I was doing, a mature buck would come along and show me how little I understood about deer behavior. Bowhunting will never be easy when pursuing pressured mature bucks, and I look forward to each season for what these bucks will teach me. Here are a few of my most memorable blunders, along with the lessons they taught me.

Early in the season in 1975, I was pursuing two large bucks that were running together, one a ten-point and the other a thirteen-point. After leaving work early on a Sunday afternoon at 4:00 P.M., I climbed up on the roof of my house to shoot my bow prior to my evening hunt. Even back then, I never practiced from the ground with my hunting equipment. My twenty-yard pin was dead on, but my thirty-five-yard pin was shooting six inches low. Since I had never used that pin while hunting before, and I was in a hurry, I decided not to adjust it; if an opportunity arose for a shot at that distance, I would just hold high. You can probably guess the rest of the story.

After I had spent about an hour sitting on a piece of two-by-four nailed into the crotch of a huge oak, deer started to pass by. This tree was located in a large area of timber between a bedding area and feeding area. Five runways ran parallel to each other within thirty-seven yards on either side of my tree. Both the ten-point and the thirteen-point calmly walked down the thirty-seven-yard runway and offered me a shot. My Bear Polar II was not the fastest bow in the world, which allowed me to watch my arrow travel toward the thirteen-point as if in slow motion and cut only hair as it passed just under his chest. I had forgotten to hold high, which caused me to miss the largest buck I had ever seen in the woods up to that time. I was sick for weeks and made a vow that I would never again enter a hunting situation knowing that my equipment was not sighted in perfectly. That problem has never occurred again. The thirteen-point buck was taken by another hunter during that year's gun season.

In 1981, I was hunting a big-woods area in northern Michigan with a very high deer population. Mature oaks were interspersed with five- to ten-year-old clear-cuts that were full of young poplars. This particular area was known for its extremely heavy gun-hunting pressure, which nearly annihilated the buck population every year. That pressure made the 140-class ten-point I had spotted early in the season seem nearly unbelievable. I wanted this buck badly. I hunted the area as much as I dared and tried every trick I could think of. Nothing worked. After a quick glimpse of the buck during the first week of October, I did not see him again until the first week of November.

The does in the area were starting to come into estrus. On an evening hunt in a big oak located at the end of a draw, I had at least a dozen does and fawns all pass directly under my tree. It was starting to get dark when the big ten-point stepped out of the poplars on the same path the other deer had taken. He followed their trail with his nose to the ground until he was twenty-eight yards away. There he stopped. For at least a minute, he stood there presenting me with several good shot opportunities. I did not shoot because I thought he would continue to follow the path the other deer had taken, in which case he would pass not ten yards from my tree. In those days, I was active in several archery leagues, so the twenty-eight-yard shot was well within my comfortable range. I just thought a ten-yard shot would be guaranteed.

Without any warning, the big buck bolted up the ridge out of bow range. From where he had been standing, he spotted a doe on the ridge that I had failed to notice with my concentration squarely focused on the buck. I never saw him again. On this hunt, I learned that if a mature buck presents me with a good shot within my comfort range, I should take it. There is so much that can happen while hunting that you have to make good on your opportunities, especially during the rut. In areas with heavy hunting pressure, it's rare to get a second chance at a mature buck.

Not all of my blunders took place over twenty years ago. Although this story is a good example of using a tarsal gland as a scent drag, I hate to tell it. On a morning hunt during the prerut in November 1997, I was hanging in my sling in a large chokecherry tree about thirty-five feet off the ground. This tree was located near the end of a forty-five-yard-long narrow opening that separated a low, swampy bedding area and a sixty-acre woodlot. The opening was about ten yards wide. Before daylight, I had dragged a tarsal gland, taken from a mature buck during the previous season's rut, from the farthest point in the opening to within fifteen yards of my tree. I then turned ninety degrees, dragged it three yards, and hung it in a bush. There was a big ten-point in the area, and I knew if he were in the area he would have to pass through the narrow opening to get to his bedding area. The only question was when. It was a picture-perfect day. The sun was out, there wasn't a cloud in the sky, and the temperature was in the high thirties. Several deer passed through the opening early in the morning and did not pay any attention to my tarsal gland scent drag. From 9:00 A.M. until nearly noon, all I saw were a couple squirrels.

Suddenly I noticed the big ten-point sneaking through the woods. As he was passing through the narrow opening at the far end, he caught the unfamiliar scent of the intruder buck. He turned and followed the scent directly toward my tree. With all the foliage in my tree gone, I was glad he kept his nose glued to the ground. The big buck momentarily stopped when he reached the spot where I had turned ninety degrees. As he turned to follow the scent trail the final three feet, I came to full draw. He took two steps and stuck his nose on the hanging tarsal gland.

Holding at full draw, I could not pull my pin down into his chest area; my mind would just not allow it. After holding for what seemed like an hour, but was probably more like ten seconds, I released my arrow only to watch as it flew right over the buck's back. It was without question the worst single event ever in all my years of bowhunting. I had missed deer, and hit deer and not recovered them, but never had I had such a perfect situation unfold and have target panic totally overcome me. I had some problems with target panic in the late seventies when shooting competitively, but never while shooting at a deer. That incident left me very humble and very aware of the reality that is bowhunting. Nothing is guaranteed or should be taken for granted.

Learning from your mistakes is part of the game. So are patience and hard work. Being able to adjust is yet another. In hunting, as in all aspects of life, nothing remains static. As you attempt to pattern deer, the deer are trying to pattern you. This is the nature of a predator-prey relationship. Deer learn from their mistakes, and if you repetitively use one tactic, they will become wise to it. A good example of this is hunting from trees in the region where I live.

In the sixties, when I started to bowhunt, a deer would rarely look up in the trees, even if you made some noise. They simply did not associate noise from trees with danger. Over the years, with more and more hunters hunting from tree stands, the deer have become accustomed to danger from above. Now it seems as though they walk through the woods looking up in the trees for lurking hunters. In pressured areas, if a hunter sets his stand only fifteen feet up in a tree, there's a good chance the deer will detect him. Because the deer have been conditioned to look for danger in trees, I've been forced to hunt higher and higher. This small adjustment has been instrumental to my consistent success.

Another example is grunt calls. When grunt calls first came on the market, they seemed to work like magic. But the more acceptance they received by hunters, the more difficult it became to get deer to respond. There are many hunters who sit in the woods and blow on their grunt calls every half hour. Mature bucks in pressured areas have heard enough calling to associate it with potential danger and will not come to it unless they see a deer, or a deer decoy, that appears to be the source of the sound. It's a good idea to refine your calling and to call only when the situation is perfect and warrants an attempt.

Always be on the lookout for ways to adjust to make yourself a better hunter. But also be aware that there are no shortcuts to success. Nothing described in this book is a shortcut. The fundamentals are postseason scouting and absolutely perfect preparation. In pressured areas, it takes a lot of time just to locate a spot that holds a mature buck. Once you find the spot, the work begins, and in order to be successful regularly, you cannot afford to make mistakes. If you do make a mistake, look for the cause of the error, correct the problem, and move on. If you are creative and open-minded, every corrected mistake should make you a better hunter.

Bowhunting is my passion, and I truly enjoy scouting and all the time I spend in the woods. I love watching deer, and I love to hunt. Deer are magnificent, very adaptive creatures, and I still have a lot to learn about them. I look forward to my continuing learning process and the opportunity and privilege to bowhunt for many years to come. I hope you have enjoyed reading about my hunting style, and that it will help you in your own learning process. Good hunting!